RACING · HISTORY

LEGENDS OF
STOCK CAR RACING

Dr. John Craft

Motorbooks International
Publishers & Wholesalers ®

First published in 1995 by Motorbooks International Publishers & Wholesalers, PO Box 2, 729 Prospect Avenue, Osceola, WI 54020 USA

Motorbooks International books are also available at discounts in bulk quantity for industrial or sales-promotional use. For details write to Special Sales Manager at the Publisher's address

Library of Congress Cataloging-in-Publication Data

Craft, John Albert.
    Legends of stock car racing/John Craft.
    Includes index.
    ISBN 0-7603-0144-1
    1. Automobile racing driver—United States—Biography. 2. Stock car racing—United States.
    I. Title.
    GV1032.A1C73   1995
    796.7'2'0922—dc20   95-9134

On the front cover: Main image: Dale Earnhardt's 1987 Monte Carlo SS; 1987 was perhaps the best year of Dale's lengthy and successful career, which includes an incredible seven Winston Cup Championships. *Craft Photo* Left inset: Davey Allison scored nineteen NASCAR victories in only six-and-a-half seasons before dying in a helicopter accident in 1993. *Craft Collection* Right inset: Richard Petty, one of the best known drivers in motorsports, in one of his trademark cowboy hats. *Craft Collection*

On the back cover: Top: Fred Lorenzen's #28 Ford Galaxie, in which "Fast Freddie" won the 1965 Daytona 500. Below: Curtis Turner, one of the sport's earliest heroes, was known for wild, dirt track broad slides and fearless impatience with any driver foolish enough to get in his way.

Printed and bound in the United States of America

Contents

Acknowledgments

*Many thanks to Jon Mauk,
author, archivist, and friend, without whose help
this effort would not have been possible.*

A replica of Donnie's Talladega is enshrined at the International Motorsports Hall of Fame in Talladega. Donnie is pictured with the late Sonny King. Craft

Prologue

Few can deny that NASCAR-style stock car racing has become the premier form of motorsports competition in the United States. While once merely a regional sport that received only grudging notice by the media, Winston Cup racing has grown to become a truly national series that enjoys television coverage of every event on the circuit.

A large part of the newfound popularity in which the NASCAR series currently basks can, of course, be attributed to the close quarters action on the track and the visceral appeal of forty-odd racing machines as they hurtle by at triple-digit velocities. Yet, as important as the mechanical aspects of stock car racing are to its overall success, it is the drivers, car owners, and mechanics behind those racing mounts that have arguably contributed the most to NASCAR's

emergence as the most popular form of motorsports in the country. And it is those often very colorful personalities who serve as the focus of this book. In the pages that follow, you will come to know thirty or so of the greatest drivers and most skillful mechanics to have ever labored in or under a racing vehicle.

Some of the racers chronicled here will be well known to even the most recently arrived NASCAR fan, while others, perhaps, will be familiar only to those who have followed the sport since its humble origins in 1948. Each legendary figure featured here has contributed to motorsports competition in significant ways, and stock car racing as we know it today would not have taken the same path without their efforts on the track and along pit road.

CHAPTER 1

Bobby, Donnie, and Davey Allison

Though Edmond and Katherine Allison bore and raised their three eldest sons, Eddie, Donnie, and Robert Arthur (Bobby) in sunny south Florida, most of the NASCAR world today remembers that trio of brothers as the founding members of the "Alabama Gang." Even so, it was in Dade County, Florida, where the boys learned how to race, and not the "Heart of Dixie"—as Alabama is sometimes called.

When Eddie, the oldest of the three Allison boys, was born in 1936, his dad was working as a service station and garage mechanic in Miami, and it's no doubt the early exposure the boys got to auto mechanics that ultimately led all three to the racetrack. Bobby made his appearance in the family next when he was born in 1937, and Donnie rounded out the racing trio in 1939. The boys spent their school years in south Florida and dabbled in a wide variety of sports. Donnie was particularly athletically inclined, and at the age of fiteen he held state of Florida championships in AAU diving and swimming.

Though the family was not rich, E.J. and Katherine made many sacrifices so that their ten children

Donnie Allison today provides technical expertise to a number of Winston Cup and Busch teams. Craft Photo

never had to want for anything. When not playing baseball and football in the back yard of their house, the boys helped Dad work on cars during afternoons and on weekends. According to Donnie, "While Dad was busy building, Eddie and I were always tinkering or tearing some engine apart. Even at home we were breaking down old bikes and putting them back together." In time, that mechanical fascination led to self-propelled transport and, ultimately, racing. Donnie got caught up in motorcycles and nearly lost his leg in a serious two-wheeled wreck when he was fifteen. During high school, Bobby bought a '38 Chevrolet. It turned out to be his first race car when his grandfather got the boys interested in racing by taking them to the early stock car races held at the Miami fairgrounds. While all three brothers eventually took a turn behind the wheel of a racing car, it was Donnie and Bobby who proved to have the greatest love—and skill—for going fast. Eddie soon took to working on their race cars, and the mechanical expertise learned at his dad's knee helped his two young brothers win many modified events at the nearby Opa-Locka, Florida, Speedway.

During the Aero-Wars of 1969 and '70, Donnie Allison campaigned a Torino Talladega for Banjo Matthews.
Craft Photo

As a young man, Bobby got a job with Carl Kiekhaefer's Mercury Outboard company. It was a natural connection since Bobby had spent many happy hours on the boat his dad kept tied up a few blocks from the family home on the Miami River. But it wasn't just the boat business that caught his attention. Race fans will recall that Kiekhaefer's Chrysler 300-based race car teams essentially had a lock on NASCAR victory lanes during the mid-fifties. According to Bobby, it was observing Kiekhaefer's racing operation that first led him to see racing as a business rather than just a hobby.

When Bobby's racing became more serious, it was only natural for his kid brother to come along on racing treks involving Bobby and older brother Eddie. In the late fifties, the Allison brothers and Red Farmer, another south Florida racer, started driving to Alabama to race because purses on the modified circuit there were better. It was in Alabama that Bobby and Donnie first established themselves as professional drivers. As mentioned, the brothers and Farmer often traveled together on the modified circuit. On one particular trip to North Carolina for a feature event, when they pulled into the track, one of the local regulars moaned, "Oh no, there's that Alabama gang."

The nickname stuck, and in later years it came to also include Bobby's young son, Davey, and Neil Bonnett.

Bobby won NASCAR's national modified championship in 1962, '63, and '64 while making selected appearances in the Grand National (nee Winston Cup) "Big Leagues." Allison's first GN appearance came in 1961—fittingly for a Florida Boy—at the second 100 mile (mi) qualifying race preceding the Daytona 500. Bobby was driving a No. 40-lettered '60 Chevrolet that day and he finished twentieth, three laps off of the pace. That performance gained him entrée to the 500 itself, and he translated a thirty-sixth starting berth into a thirty-first-place finish. Though young Bobby didn't know it at the time, it would be sixteen more years before he would be able to park a race car in the 500's victory lane (when in 1978 he won the race in a Bud Moore Thunderbird). All told, Allison started four GN races in 1961 without much luck. By season's end he had won just $650 in GN prize money.

Allison returned to the Grand National ranks in 1965, this time behind the wheel of a Ford. He fared a bit better that season and turned in three top ten finishes. It was in 1966 that Bobby stunned the racing world by winning three Grand National events in

Allison's Big T was often one of the fastest on the track. Here it sits on the outside pole at the Firecracker 400 in 1969. Craft Photo

Bobby Allison holds the distinction of winning a Grand National race in a 1970 Holman and Moody prepared Boss 302 Mustang. That win came in 1971 when NASCAR combined the Grand National and Grand American divisions at a handful of races. Craft Collection

a home-built small-block-powered Chevrolet. Win number one came at Oxford, Maine, where he put his short track background to work winning a 100mi event on the .333mi oval. Tiny Lund and Richard Petty rounded out the top three that day. Allison's two other wins in the home-built car came at short track events at Islip, New York, and Beltsville, Maryland.

It was at Bowman Gray Stadium in the race following his third win that Bobby established a reputation for fearlessness. During the event, he got into an on-track shoving match with veteran fender-rubber Curtis Turner, who had just returned to NASCAR after being banned for five years by circuit president Bill France. Turner, who'd earned the nickname "Pops" early in his career for his fondness of popping cars right off of the racetrack, hooked Allison's bumper on lap eight and spun the youngster out. Unfazed, Allison charged back, and soon the two cars were hammering each other. Turner lost the next round and spun out himself. He then crept around the track, lying in wait for Allison's Chevrolet, and the two crashed into each other for the next ten laps—even during yellow flag laps. Each spun out the other several more times until finally track officials ejected both from the race. Each was fined $100 for their on-track antics and Junior Johnson, Turner's car owner, came close to firing him for the melee. The incident was ultimately featured in a *Sports Illustrated* article about the race.

Bobby Allison's performance in 1966 earned him a seat in Bud Moore's factory-backed Mercury at the beginning of the 1967 season. When that relationship soured, Allison went back to driving independently backed Chevrolets. After winning a short track race in one of the Chevrolets at Savannah, he was named to drive the Cotton Owens' factory-backed Dodge that David Pearson had vacated to fill Fred Lorenzen's seat at Holman and Moody. It was Allison's first big-time driving contract. Nine races later that new combination was in victory lane at Birmingham. When Owens decided not to campaign the team Dodge at a race on the Northern tour, he gave Allison permission to run his old Chevrolet at Oxford, Maine, a race that he ultimately won. Though Owens signed off on the deal, his corporate sponsors were outraged that a team driver would win for another manufacturer, so Bobby was given his walking papers. He next showed up behind the wheel of a

Fairlane that recently retired Ford driver Fred Lorenzen had persuaded Fomoco to let him campaign "his way." Lorenzen was impressed with Allison's smoothness on the track and said so. With Jake Elder providing mechanical support, Lorenzen and Allison entered the car in the American 500 in Rockingham. David Pearson, Ford's new H&M driver, sat on the pole for the race and Allison qualified third. Even so, during the race it was all Allison. He led the race on six occasions for a total of 164 laps. When the checkered flag fell, he was a full lap ahead of second-place finisher Pearson. His performance that day helped secure a factory-backed Ford ride with dealer Bondy Long's team for 1968.

While Bobby was having his up-and-down year on the circuit in 1967, younger brother Donnie was running hard for rookie of the year honors. Like Bobby before him, Donnie had run the modified circuit for a number of years before trying his hand at Grand National competition. He had made his first GN start in 1966 and returned a creditable ninth-place finish at Rockingham in an independently backed Chevrolet. In 1967, he drove a series of Chevrolets, Dodges, and Fords to four top-five finishes and the coveted top rookie honor. It earned him a factory-backed ride in

Not many people took American Motors' racing effort seriously during the mid-seventies, until Bobby Allison put a Matador in victory lane at the Southern 500, that is. Craft Photo

Though it may come as a surprise to some, Bobby Allison drove for Holman and Moody in 1971. He campaigned this red-and-gold Cyclone for that fabled Ford factory racing team that year. Craft Collection

Banjo Matthews' Torino for 1968, and when that season began, both he and big brother Bobby were part of Ford's "Going Thing." It was Donnie who found victory first that season when he dominated the Carolina 500 at Rockingham in Matthews' No. 27 Ford.

Bobby was right on his bumper in second place at the wheel of the Chevrolet he had gone back to after leaving the Bondy Long Ford team. Bobby's first win of 1968 came a few weeks later at Islip, New York, where he beat the factory-backed teams with his independently sponsored Chevy.

Donnie stayed with Banjo and Ford for 1969 while Bobby found work at the wheel of Mario Rossi's Dodge. With the Aero-Wars, the manufacturers' aerodynamic battles, in full swing, Bobby and Donnie proved to be two of the best Aero-warriors for their respective marques. Donnie drove long-nosed Torino Talladegas to victory in the National 500 at Charlotte and to nine other top-five finishes. Bobby notched five victories and rounded out the top five at six others. Team affiliations remained unchanged for both brothers in 1970, though by that time Bobby's Charger 500 had sprouted wings to become a Dodge Daytona. Both Allisons ran in the fastest pack all season. Bobby won the Atlanta 500 in March, for example, and Donnie countered with a victory at Bristol, Tennessee, the next step on the circuit. Donnie was the family superspeedway champ that season with two other long track wins in the World 600 and the Firecracker 400. Bobby contented

Bobby Allison always favored General Motors-powered race cars, which is why, no doubt, his first efforts as a team owner took him back to Chevrolet power. This is the car he provided Hut Stricklin shortly after becoming a team owner. Craft Collection

himself with short track wins at Bristol and Hampton, Virginia.

As race fans of that era will recall, the bottom fell out of factory-backed racing in the years from 1970 to 1972. Ford was the first to fold its tent in 1970 and Mopar pulled up stakes not long after. When that happened both Allisons reverted to fielding independently sponsored cars and both dabbled briefly in Indy car racing. Donnie began the 1971 season with Banjo again but had moved to the Wood brothers by year's end to field their Cyclones. Bobby started out on his own in a Dodge. When a salary dispute resulted in David Pearson's departure from the Holman & Moody team, Bobby once again filled the seat (as he had in 1967) that Pearson had just vacated. The Holman and Moody car picked up red-and-gold No. 12 Coca-Cola sponsorship with Bobby's arrival and immediately started winning.

Bobby's first outing in the car came at Talladega in the Winston 500, where he got a close-up and personal view of the back bumper of brother Donnie's Mercury as it crossed the finish line first. Bobby returned the favor three races later when he lead Donnie across the stripe at the World 600. Bobby won ten more times that season, six of which he scored in the H&M Mercury. Among the wins were superspeedway triumphs at Dover, Michigan, Talladega, and Darlington, where he notched his first Southern 500 title.

Bobby backed up his eleven victories in 1971 with ten more in 1972, when he returned "home" to his first love—Chevrolets. The Bow Tie car in question was backed by Richard Howard and prepared by Junior Johnson. The success that Allison had that year was the first taste of the victories Chevrolet would enjoy in NASCAR racing over the next two decades.

Throughout his long career, "Bobby A" drove for both himself and other teams. During the seventies he was successfully paired with Bud Moore's Ford operation and won several major races for the team, including the 1978 Daytona 500. The Daytona Racing Archives

During the Aero-Wars, Bobby and Donnie were on opposite sides of the battle line. Donnie drove a Talladega while Bobby campaigned at Daytona. Donnie won that *particular sibling rivalry, scoring more wins than his big brother during the same period. The Daytona Racing Archives*

Allison's Coca-Cola-sponsored Monte Carlo notched the first win for that soon-to-be-famous body style at Atlanta, when he edged out A.J. Foyt's Wood Brothers' Cyclone in the Atlanta 500. He backed up the Atlanta win with another in the Dixie 500 to be the king of that Georgia track in 1972. He also scored his second straight Southern 500 win and seven other Winston Cup victories. His on-track efforts resulted in a second place finish in that season's points standing, just 120 or so back of champion Richard Petty.

While Bobby's NASCAR star burned bright during 1972, Donnie's was dimmed somewhat. He started ten races that season, for both Roger Penske (in an AMC Matador) and for Bud Moore (in his small-block-powered Ford), but was only able to produce two top-ten finishes.

Donnie remained active in the GN ranks for several more seasons and campaigned a number of Chevrolets for several different teams. During that time, he scored three more wins, including the 1977 Talladega 500, which he won with the relief driving help of Darrell Waltrip. Donnie's final Winston Cup win came at the Dixie 500 in November 1978. It was unfortunately marred by a NASCAR scoring error that, for a while, relegated him to second place. When NASCAR officials realized their mistake, Allison was awarded the victory. Donnie continued to race until the mid-eighties. He finished his career with ten total Grand National/Winston Cup wins.

Though Donnie's career tapered off after the factory-backed racing era ended, Bobby's star continued to rise. In 1973, he left Junior Johnson's employ and set out on his own in a Coca-Cola-sponsored Chevelle, scoring two wins. He continued on his own with a Chevrolet-based team in 1974, but at midseason he signed on with Roger Penske to drive a red, white, and blue Matador. "Nash's" factory-backed racing effort didn't generate much respect, even with famed former driver and Trans-Am championship-winning team owner Penske at the helm. Allison quickly changed that and by the end of the year he had the Matador finishing in the top five.

He even parked the car in victory lane at the season closing L.A. Times 500 at Riverside but was subsequently fined more than $9,000 when a postrace tear-down revealed illegal lifters.

When the 1975 season began, Allison somewhat redeemed himself by winning—cleanly—the season-opening Winston Riverside 500 for AMC's second WC win. He stopped people from laughing at the little red, white, and blue car altogether at Daytona, where he finished second at the 500 behind Benny Parsons. AMC credibility was assured when Allison drove his No. 16 car to victory at Darlington in the Rebel 400. He made jaws drop later that year by winning the always tough Southern 500 for a clean sweep of Darlington by a Rambler.

When team owner Penske switched to Cam 2-backed Mercurys in 1976, so did team driver Allison. But by 1977 he was back in an AMC, this one fielded by his own Alabama-based racing team. In 1978, Bobby signed with famed mechanic and team owner Bud Moore, and for the next three seasons he drove refrigerator-white No. 15 Fords and Mercurys. It proved to be a successful partnership. Together, he and Moore's Spartanburg, South Carolina-based team won fourteen series events, including Allison's first triumph at the Daytona 500. It was while driving for Moore in the 1979 Daytona 500 that Bobby and Donnie formed a wrestling tag team of sorts on Daytona's back stretch. Donnie and Cale Yarborough had been battling for position on the track for a number of laps when, with just fifty laps remaining in the event, Cale's Junior Johnson-prepped Olds slid into Donnie's Hoss Ellington car. The two went careening off into the back stretch grass and ground to a halt. Seeing the shunt, Bobby stopped to check on his baby brother's condition. And that's when the

Davey Allison continued the family's NASCAR winning ways after he teamed up with Robert Yates and began to drive the Havoline Thunderbird. Craft Collection

Davey Allison would no doubt have been a Winston Cup champion like his dad had he not been killed in a freak helicopter accident at Talladega. Craft Collection

fists started flying. Showing much the same style that he had displayed when banging on Curtis Turner years before, Bobby waded into the battle with Cale and the whole fracas was captured live on nationwide television. The sanctioning body was appalled, and several races later all drivers involved in the "bout" were forced to publicly "kiss and make up." Allison went on to win for Moore at Talladega (in the Winston 500) and at three other venues that year. In 1980, that duo found further superspeedway success by winning the Firecracker 400.

In 1981, Bobby went back to GM-powered race cars, this time Pontiacs and Chevrolets built by Harry Ranier—the same team that his young son Davey would drive for several years later. The championship race that year was a tight one and Allison and Darrell Waltrip were the top two in points. Ultimately, Allison would lose the title to "DW" by a mere fifty-three points. In 1982, Allison won his second Daytona 500, this time in a Di-Gard team Buick. He was the king of Daytona that year as he also finished first in the Firecracker 400. As in 1981, the driving championship came down to a two-man race, Allison and Waltrip. Allison's eight victories and six top-ten finishes, while impressive, once again came up short to Waltrip's twelve and five, respectively. Waltrip was champ again.

The planets finally lined up for Bobby Allison and his championship quest in 1983. Still with Di-Gard, Allison campaigned Miller High Life Pontiacs during

Daytona was one of Davey's favorite tracks. He won the Daytona 500 in 1992. Craft Photo

Though only on the Winston Cup tour a handful of seasons, Davey Allison was able to win nineteen Winston Cup races with the help of his lightning-quick pit crew.
Craft Collection

his championship season. His first of six wins that year came in the Richmond 400. Allison notched his fourth Southern 500 in 1983 on his way to scoring 4,667 Winston Cup points—a too-close-for-comfort Thirty-three more than old rival Darrell Waltrip amassed. The points race was so tight that year, in fact, the championship wasn't decided until the end of the last race at Riverside. Following the checkered flag, Allison, his crew chief Gary Nelson, and team engine builder Robert Yates were all smiles. After twenty-two years of trying, Bobby Allison was NASCAR's driving champion.

Allison continued to run the circuit until a horrifying wreck at Pocono nearly took his life in 1988. After a long and painful recovery, he finally returned to the NASCAR fold as a car owner. The eighty-four victories that Bobby Allison scored in his twenty-seven-year driving career place him third on the overall NASCAR win list behind Richard Petty and David Pearson.

In addition to his other triumphs, Bobby also scored a number of off-track successes during his racing days, most notable among them being his two sons, Davey and Clifford. Born in south Florida the same year as his dad's first NASCAR start in 1961, Davey Allison grew up on the NASCAR circuit. It was only natural, then, for him to want to follow in his fa-

ther's footsteps and become a racing driver in his own right. At first, father Bobby made Davey pay his dues with shop work, but finally Davey was allowed to go modified racing in 1979. By 1985, young Davey was sure that he was ready to face the challenges of big league Winston Cup competition. He made his first start that year at his hometown track, Talladega. Davey drove a Chevrolet for Hoss Ellington that day and showed promise by finishing tenth in his first superspeedway run. Davey made two more starts that season for Ellington and made five for Sadler Racing the following year before jumping into the Rookie of the Year race in 1987.

Davey's team for his first full year of Winston Cup competition was almost part of the family. Team co-owner Harry Ranier had previously provided cars for Davey's dad, and the team's engine builder, Robert Yates, was the man who had "powered" Bobby to his 1983 WC Championship. With Havoline as the major sponsor, Davey's Thunderbird that year also carried the No. 28 that his dad had campaigned at one point in his career. At Daytona, Davey qualified second, only the second time in NASCAR history that a rookie driver had started on the front row of stock car racing's "Super Bowl." Unfortunately, Davey ran into bad luck during the race and finished a distant twenty-seventh. But victory was in the offing three

Davey returning to battle in 1987. Craft Photo

months later, and what better place for Davey to cinch his first WC win than Talladega. Davey qualified third for the Winston 500 that year and then led much of the way to win a race that had boasted the fastest starting field in history. (Bill Elliott sat on the pole with a qualifying speed of 212.809mph.) Later that same month Davey won a second time at Dover and ultimately won Rookie of the Year accolades with ease. He seemed destined for certain super-stardom as a NASCAR driver

The 1988 race year began on a story book note at Daytona where Davey battled for victory with his dad in the closing laps of the 500 classic. The father and son duo had qualified third and second (respectively), and in the event's waning stages it became apparent that the race was theirs to decide among themselves. The two-car-length victory Bobby scored over Davey was his third in the 500 and the first such father-and-son finish since Lee and Richard Petty had finished nose-to-tail at Heidelberg Speedway in 1960. After the race Bobby said, "It was really good to be in

Robert Yates' shop is located just west of downtown Charlotte. That's where he maintained the fleet of Thunderbirds Davey drove. Craft Photo

Donnie Allison (left) and Cale Yarborough (right) were two of the hottest drivers in NASCAR during the 1968 to 1970 seasons. The Daytona Racing Archives

front. It was a great feeling to look back and see somebody you feel is the best coming up driver and know it's your son. It's a very special feeling and it's hard to put into words."

Davey avoided any hint of NASCAR's traditional sophomore jinx and went on to score fifteen more top-ten finishes in his second year on the circuit, including wins at Michigan and Richmond. Along the way he became one of the most popular drivers on the circuit, both with fans and his on-track rivals.

When Robert Yates took over the Ranier-Lundy operation in 1989, Allison stayed on as team driver and his black, gold, and white Thunderbirds continued to run at the front of the pack. He won two times that year (the Winston 500 and the Firecracker 400) and twice more the next season. In 1991, Davey began a serious run at the Winston Cup championship and stretched his win total to thirteen with five more victories. He won the World 600 in Charlotte in May, he showed roadrace skill in June when he won the Sears Point race, and he finished out the season with wins at Michigan, Rockingham, and Phoenix.

The 1992 race year brought five more victories, including a popular triumph in the Daytona 500. While his dad had tried seventeen years before winning his first 500, young Davey had accomplished

the feat in just eight. Davey also won again at Talladega that year, making him one of the most successful drivers to ever run on that 2.66mi oval. At year's end, Davey was third in the points standings, just sixty-three behind that year's champ, Alan Kulwicki. Though 1992 had been a successful year on the track for Davey, it also held great personal tragedy for the Allison family when Davey's younger brother, Clifford, was killed in a practice crash at Michigan.

With fan and family support, Davey headed into 1993 hoping for happier days and perhaps his first Winston Cup championship. Tragically, it was not to be. On July 12, 1993, while Allison was trying to land his helicopter in the infield at Talladega, a freak accident caused the chopper to spin out of control. Though charter Alabama gang member Red Farmer (Allison's passenger) survived, Davey was pronounced dead at 7 a.m. the next day. The nineteen career victories he had scored in an all-too-short six-and-a-half full-time seasons place Davey twenty-third on the all-time win list, where he is tied with Fonty Flock, Speedy Thompson, Buddy Baker, and Neil Bonnett—another member of the Alabama Gang who tragically lost *his* life during practice for the 1994 Daytona 500.

Buck and Buddy Baker

It was while Elzie Wylie "Buck" Baker, Sr., was employed as a Charlotte, North Carolina, bus driver that he decided he could be a race car driver. After all, he already drove for a living. Had done it most of his life, in fact. And better yet, cars on a race track all went in the same direction. There'd be no need to worry about oncoming traffic or other drivers darting out of side roads. Heck, racing would be easy. Perhaps it was for someone with the natural talent of Buck Baker, a forty-six-time Grand National winner and 1956 and 1957 NASCAR GN driving champion.

Like many of his contemporaries on the early NASCAR circuit, Buck Baker was raised on a farm in the Carolinas. Born on March 4, 1919, near Chester, South Carolina, Baker in his younger days was much fonder of four-legged things than anything with wheels. Farming filled his early years, and it was a wild and uncontrollable bull calf his mom had named Buck that provided the nickname that Baker has had all his life. You see, according to Baker's mother, he was just as wild and untamed as was that bull calf. In fact, Baker says that everyone

Before embarking on a career in racing, Buck Baker held many jobs, including moonshine runner and Trailways bus driver. The Daytona Racing Archives

who knew him during those years was sure he'd be dead before the advanced age of twenty-one.

Part of that unruliness took the form of running moonshine for his cousin. As luck would have it, the police tried to stop him on his very first delivery and he had to outrun them to stay out of jail. That's when Baker decided he was pretty good behind the wheel. In addition to running 'shine, Baker also got by during the Depression by working in a bakery, selling cars, and working for the CCC (Civilian Conservation Corps) planting trees. Ultimately World War II and Navy service took him away from South Carolina for an extended sabbatical in Maryland—where he continued to run 'shine in his spare time for his barracks mates. It seems that not even the Navy could harness Baker's wild ways.

After his hitch in the Navy, Baker and his family (wife Margaret and son Elzie Wylie "Buddy" Baker, Jr.) settled in Charlotte, where Buck found work as a Trailways bus driver. But even then Baker was an unrequited free spirit. He's fond of telling the story, for example, of the time when he and the passengers

Buck Baker was the Grand National driving champion in 1956. He drove Chrysler 300s for team owner Carl Kiekhaefer that year. He's shown here with teammates Herb Thomas and Speedy Thompson (left to right). The Daytona Racing Archives

on the bus decided to take in a big square dance in Chester—which wasn't the final stop on his run that day. When the bus came up overdue, his Trailways supervisors became understandably concerned and feared that perhaps he'd run off the road. The State Highway Patrol was notified and began to search for Baker and his errant bus. When he finally pulled into the station hours behind schedule with a bus full of drunk and singing passengers, the dispatcher wanted to fire him on the spot. It was only the exhortations of the well-pleased—and regular—passengers that saved his job.

As we've mentioned, it was while driving the bus that Baker first got the idea to drive a race car. He was twenty-seven at the time—far older than most other drivers on the circuit in an era where most retired well before their fortieth birthdays. But even so, he quickly made a name for himself on the dirt tracks around Charlotte. Baker's first race was in 1946, but

it wasn't until seven years later that he decided to run the Grand National circuit full time.

During his early years of racing Baker campaigned a variety of makes for both himself and other owners. His first Grand National win came in 1952, when he outdistanced Lee Petty in a 100mi dirt track event in Columbia, South Carolina. But it wasn't until he signed on as a team driver for Carl Kiekhaefer's Chrysler 300 Mercury Outboard team that Baker really made his mark in the Grand National division. Kiekhaefer was the most powerful and resourceful team owner in NASCAR at the time. Rather than participating in the sport out of love for it, Kiekhaefer had decided to go NASCAR racing as the result of a cold-blooded business decision. It occurred to him that a good number of potential customers for his company's outboard boat engines liked to attend stock car races. With that kind of captive audience in one place for hours at a time, it only

Buck's oldest son Buddy followed in Dad's footsteps to become a NASCAR star in his own right. The Daytona Racing Archives

made sense to sponsor a team of race cars that could be emblazoned with the corporation's logo. And since the cars that won got the most attention from the fans, Kiekhaefer's cars would just have to win—everything.

To achieve this goal, Kiekhaefer spent huge sums of 1950s dollars. The team raced Chrysler 300s because they were the fastest and most powerful (the first American cars to feature 300 stock horsepower) automobiles being made at the time. Because it was risky to rely solely on just one car and driver to win a race, Kiekhaefer hired several, and he always tried to hire the best pilots available. Of course that required paying the highest salaries, and that's exactly what he did. It's been said that Kiekhaefer drivers were paid in excess of $40,000 a year to drive for the team. And that, in an era where $4,000 would buy the plushest Cadillac (or Chrysler 300) in the showroom floor, was basically all the money in the world. Of course Kiekhaefer expected a return on his investment, just as any businessman would. To gain that return, he ruled his teams with an iron fist. Curfews were strictly enforced the night before a race, and Kiekhaefer would sometimes segregate drivers from

During the Aero-Wars, Buddy drove Dodges for Cotton Owens and Ray Fox. He's shown here in 1970 with his Cotton Owens-prepared Daytona. Though he spent most of his time during the Aero-Wars getting a close look at the back bumper of his Talladega and Spoiler II rivals, he later won several major races after joining Bud Moore's Ford team. The Daytona Racing Archives

their wives and girl-friends to keep them focused on the job at hand—winning races. Kiekhaefer even went so far as to hire soil and weather specialists to evaluate the track and atmospheric conditions on race day to better prepare the team's cars.

Though Kiekhaefer's rigid discipline earned him the nickname "Iron Fist," it certainly worked. In 1955, his first year on the circuit, team drivers won twenty-two Grand National victories, $37,779 in prize money, and the national driving championship for Tim Flock.

Even so, Kiekhaefer wasn't satisfied. The following season he set out to win even more of the races. Doing so, in his opinion, required hiring Buck Baker, Flock's archrival on the circuit in 1955. For the 1956 season, Baker was paired with Fonty Flock, Herb Thomas, Speedy Thompson, Tim Flock, and Frank "Rebel" Mundy, who replaced Tim at midseason.

Tim Flock won the first race of the '56 season at Hickory and led all but sixteen laps of the 80mi dirt track affair. Baker's first victory came at Phoenix in January 1956. By season's end Baker had collected thirteen more checkered flags and sixteen other top five finishes, $34,076 in prize money, and his first Grand National driving championship. At one point during the season, the Kiekhaefer juggernaut won an incredible sixteen races in a row. Unfortunately for Kiekhaefer, his team's on-track success did not translate into the goodwill with the fans he had desired. In fact, their reaction was quite the opposite and they made their sentiments known with jeers, by throwing bottles, and by not attending races. NASCAR's Big Bill France was equally displeased, especially when the winning streak caused gate receipts to fall off. Pressure from the sanctioning body in the form of frequent tear-downs and technical inspections (which the cars passed with flying colors), coupled with the unfavorable fan reaction, persuaded Kiekhaefer to seek advertising exposure elsewhere. In 1957, he pulled out of the sport altogether.

Thus out of a ride, Baker signed on as a Chevrolet team driver for 1957. The Bow Tie division of General Motors had scored its first NASCAR win two years before when the all-new 265ci, overhead-valve "mouse" motor had been introduced. General Motors team manager Frankie Del Roy had tapped Hugh Babb of Atlanta to head up Chevrolet's NASCAR efforts for '57, and Babb jumped at the chance to sign the reigning series champion. Other drivers on the General's payroll that year included Speedy Thompson, Rex White, Jack Smith, and Johnny Beauchamp.

Then, as now, the first big race of the season was at Daytona, and Baker drove his fuel-injected '57 Chevy to creditable fourth-place finish. A pair of dirt track second-place finishes came next before Baker's first '57 win at Hillsboro, North Carolina. With the help of chief mechanic Bud Moore, Baker won nine more times that season, including the 101.2mi road

While still driving Dodges in 1970, Buddy Baker became the first man to crack the 200mph barrier in this R&D Dodge Daytona. Part of the secret of Baker's 200+ mph record run was his car's rear wing. Not only did it provide 600+ lbs of positive down force, it also enhanced lateral stability. Craft Photo

race at Watkins Glen. There's little doubt that Baker's earliest road race training—running 'shine—helped immensely as he won the first NASCAR road course event at the fabled New York state track. At the end of the fifty-three-event season, Baker was once again NASCAR's Grand National driving champion, the first back-to-back champion. Chevrolet might have won its first manufacturer's championship, had the award existed at the time.

Baker stayed with Chevrolet for '58. When Chevrolet took part in the charade of withdrawing from factory-backed motorsports (in response to the AMA ban that GM had secretly engineered to keep Ford from winning), Baker was listed as his car's owner on all official NASCAR entry forms. The back door to Chevrolet's racing division remained open, however, and Baker was one of the beneficiaries of the corporation's clandestine largess. He finished first in three GN events that year, and was in the top five at twenty others, but that was still good enough for a second place in the season points race behind Lee Petty.

At the close of the Aero-Wars, Buddy Baker signed on to drive a "wingless" Dodge for Petty Engineering. Here he (11) leads A.J. Foyt (21), Pete Hamilton, Richard Petty, *and Bobby Allison in the '71 Daytona 500.* Craft Collection

Baker continued to race for a number of years, but he never again achieved the success he'd enjoyed during the '56 and '57 seasons. After his last race in 1971, he'd racked up forty-six GN wins and $325,570 in earnings, and is eleventh on NASCAR's all-time winner's list.

Buck Baker also made another significant contribution to racing in the form of his eldest son, Buddy.

Buck Baker, two time Grand National champion, today runs his own NASCAR driving school at Charlotte. Craft Photo

Starting with his first race on the circuit in 1959, the amiable and imposing (at 6ft, 5in) Baker, Jr., was a force in the Grand National ranks for more than two decades. Buddy spent his first years on the circuit campaigning Chevrolets and Fords, but he is perhaps better known for the lightning-fast Dodges he drove for legendary mechanic Ray Fox in the late sixties. Buddy's first win came in 1967 at the National 500 in Charlotte at the helm of a Hemi-powered Ray Fox Charger. He quickly developed the reputation as a wide-open-throttle driver who loved high speeds and superspeedways. Baker's second win came at the next race in Charlotte, the World 600, where he again piloted a No. 3 Ray Fox Dodge to victory.

In 1969, Baker's Chargers became even slippier with the addition of Charger 500 aero-aides, including, by the end of the season, the radical beaks and wings of the Dodge Daytona. Baker turned in nine top five finishes in his day-glo No. 6 Cotton Owens Charger that year, and seemingly had the season-ending Texas 500 superspeedway race in the bag until a momentary lapse (when he ran into the back of James Hylton's Daytona) in the late going, which sent him to the garage.

The 1970 race year saw the Chryco Aero-fleet's greatest success following the reduction of Ford's racing budget by new chief exec Lido Iacocca. Buddy Baker took advantage of his winged car's speed and won the 1970 Southern 500 at Darlington in his Daytona. He lead-footed that same Cotton Owens-prepped Aero-warrior to five more 1970

top-five finishes. He also became the first man in history to break the 200mph barrier by driving a Dodge R&D Daytona around Talladega at 200.447mph in March 1970.

In 1971, Baker became a team driver for Petty Enterprises and campaigned a Coke bottle-bodied No. 11 Charger for the next two seasons. Along the way, he won the Rebel 400 ('71), the World 600 ('72), and the Texas 500 ('72). All were superspeed-way-type races, which Baker thrived on.

In '73, Baker drove a K&K Charger to two victories, including another World 600 triumph. 1975 was Baker's best year for wins as he amassed four. The first of those was the Winston 600 at Talladega, where he scored one of the first superspeedway wins for team owner Bud Moore's small-block-powered Ford. (At the time, small-block engines were the wave of the future in NASCAR, and Moore was one of the first to make them work.) Baker was the king of Talladega that year as he won the Talladega 500 in August, again at the wheel of the Norris Industries-backed Ford. He closed the year with a win at Atlanta and another in road course action at the season finale in Riverside, California.

Baker won one more time for Moore in 1976, winning at Talladega in the Winston, making it three in a row for Baker, Moore, and Ford at the World's Fastest Racetrack.

Baker drove General Motors products for the balance of his career, earning his final six victories (of the nineteen that place him twenty-fifth on the all-time win list). Most notable among them was the 1980 Daytona 500 win he scored in Harry Ranier's black and silver No. 28 Oldsmobile.

It's rare for a father and son to choose racing as a way of life and rarer still for both to become legends on the circuit. But that's just what happened with Buck and Buddy Baker.

Buddy Baker joined the ranks of media commentators following his retirement from racing. Craft Photo

CHAPTER 3

Dale Earnhardt

The Intimidator, the Dominator, Ironhead, and on occasion, a number of other nicknames unprintable here, have all been used to describe Ralph Dale Earnhardt, Jr. during his incredibly successful NASCAR career. But as long as people continue calling him a winner immediately following a Winston Cup race, Dale Earnhardt probably won't concern himself with all the other names.

Earnhardt was born into a racing family on April 29, 1951. His father, Ralph, Sr., was a hard charger on the modified circuit (and occasional starter in the Grand National ranks) who was NASCAR's national modified champ in 1956. So it's probably only natural that young Dale also set his sights on becoming a racer. Though his formal education did not continue beyond middle school, Earnhardt received advanced "degrees" in driving on the modified circuit.

Dale Earnhardt's first Winston Cup start was anything but auspicious. It came in 1975 at the World 600, just down the road a piece from his home in Kannapolis, North Carolina. His "mount" that day was a Coke bottle-bodied '74 Dodge Charger that belonged to journeyman racer Ed Negre. Earnhardt qualified the No. 8 car thirty-third that day

Over the years Earnhardt has developed a reputation for rough driving that fans don't always appreciate. Here he receives the grandstand's boos at Charlotte in 1987. Craft Photo

and finished in twenty-second place—forty-five laps behind race winner Richard Petty. Immediately behind Earnhardt in twenty-third was an independent driver named Richard Childress. It would not be the last time that the two would be "paired" in a NASCAR stock car race.

Earnhardt made no further forays into the NASCAR ranks that year and until 1979, never ran more than five races a season. In between those infrequent early rides, Earnhardt made a name for himself on the same Modified Sportsman tour that his dad had dominated two decades earlier. Earnhardt's first Winston Cup break came in 1978, thanks to Willy T. Ribbs. At the time, Ribbs was a promising driver in the sports car ranks and the most prominent black racer in the country. Humpy Wheeler, the world-class showman and general manager of the Charlotte Motor Speedway, made arrangements for Ribbs to run in the World 600 that year. A Bud Moore Ford (the same one that Buddy Baker had driven to Talladega victories in '75 and '76) was lined up, and Will Cronkite signed on as team owner.

Everything was in place, in fact, except Ribbs. Though Willy was eventually located by the Charlotte

Dale Earnhardt's best year on the circuit came in 1987 when he won eleven races. His car that year was this blue-and-yellow Wrangler Monte Carlo SS. Craft Photo

police driving the wrong way down a one-way street, he never made it to the CMS to shake down the Ford, and ultimately Cronkite replaced him with Earnhardt. Earnhardt qualified the No. 96 car in the twenty-eighth spot, and finished seventeenth. He earned his first top-five Winston Cup finish later that season, driving a Rod Osterland Chevrolet to a fourth place finish in the Dixie 500 at Atlanta. It was a harbinger of great things to come for the partnership.

In 1979, Osterland and Earnhardt were a team again. In their first outing at Riverside, Earnhardt qualified the yellow-and-blue No. 2 team Monte Carlo tenth. Unfortunately, engine trouble sidelined the effort for a DNF. Six races later, though, Earnhardt

scored his first NASCAR win at the Southeastern 500 at Bristol. Earnhardt started ninth but turned in a dominating win over Bobby Allison, who took second in Bud Moore's Ford. All told, Earnhardt and Osterland made eighteen starts that season, and in addition to the Bristol win, had two seconds, seven top tens, and won the Rookie of the Year title. Earnhardt was on his way.

For many Rookie of the Year winners, their second year on the circuit is often a letdown. So common is this phenomenon that it has a name: the sophomore jinx. If Earnhardt ever heard of that supposed jinx, he obviously paid no attention. In 1980, he and Osterland were again a team and they did

After having been outrun by Ford's slippery Thunderbirds in 1985 and 1986, Chevrolet grafted a new nose cone and a fastback roofline onto their squared-off Monte Carlo. The car, basically a recreation of the Torino Talladegas Ralph Moody developed in 1969, was an immediate success. Craft Photo

Earnhardt and the late Alan Kulwicki go at it in 1987. Craft Photo

the seemingly impossible by winning the Winston Cup national championship in Earnhardt's second (official) year on the circuit. It was an incredible feat that's never been duplicated. Earnhardt began the season with a second at Riverside and a fourth in the Daytona 500. Win number one that year came in the Atlanta 500, and Earnhardt made it two in a row two weeks later with his second Bristol victory. Earnhardt's No. 2 Chevrolet won three more times that season and recorded fourteen other top-five finishes in winning his first NASCAR title.

Perhaps Earnhardt's sophomore jinx actually happened in 1981, his third season on the tour. Still teamed with Osterland and backed by a new sponsor, Wrangler, all signs at the start of the year were positive. Even so, at mid-season, Osterland sold the team and Earnhardt began driving for Richard Childress, who had recently retired from driving to field

Part of Earnhardt's success is the incredibly fast work his pit crew is capable of. They call themselves the Flying Aces. Craft Photo

Earnhardt's Monte Carlos picked up Goodwrench black racing livery in the late eighties and looked even more intimidating. Craft Photo

When Monte Carlos were phased out, Earnhardt began
campaigning Chevrolet Luminas for Richard Childress.
Craft Photo

Earnhardt won the WC championship for Rod Osterland.
He drove #2 yellow-and-blue Monte Carlos for Osterland

like this one. Craft Photo

Though it may come as a shock to his Chevrolet fans, "Ironhead" at one time campaigned Fords for Bud Moore. Craft Photo

Above and next page
For 1995, Dale Earnhardt returned to the Monte Carlo that brought him such success during the seventies. Graced with sleek lines and favored by the NASCAR rules book, Earnhardt and his Monte Carlo are sure to visit victory lane. Craft Collection

his own team. Earnhardt drove Childress' No. 3 Pontiac in the last eleven races of the season and turned in two top-five finishes for the team.

In 1982 and 1983, Earnhardt drove Fords, campaigning the No. 15 Wrangler Thunderbird in a two-year association with famed Fomoco team owner Bud Moore. He won the 1982 Rebel 300, and in 1983, he won for Ford at Nashville and Talladega.

While Moore had hopes of sticking with his aggressive young driver, Chevrolet was courting Earnhardt heavily during his time with Moore, and in 1983, Earnhardt returned to Childress' operation. He has never looked back. Since re-upping with Childress, Earnhardt has won fifty times. In that number

are: seven wins at Darlington; six at Talladega; four at Charlotte; four at Atlanta; four at Michigan; and two at Daytona. In fact, just about the only major race Earnhardt has yet to win is the Daytona 500. Even more impressive are the seven Winston Cup championships he has won during that time.

His best year with the team to date came in 1987, when he posted wins at eleven events and finished in the top ten at thirteen others. Earnhardt is currently sixth on NASCAR's all-time win list and is tied with "King" Richard Petty for national championship wins. And he's likely to better both of these marks in the seasons to come.

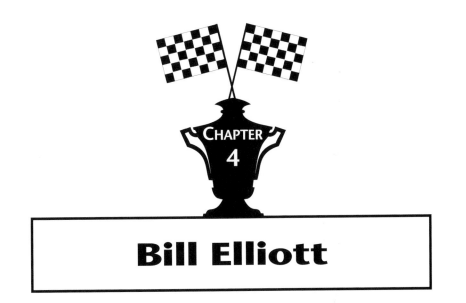

Chapter 4

Bill Elliott

You might say that Bill Elliott was anything but awesome in his first NASCAR Winston Cup stock car race. The year was 1976 and Elliott was a fresh-faced twenty-one-year-old from Dawsonville, Georgia. Elliott's first race was the Carolina 500 in Rockingham, and the No. 9 Ford his father had provided for young Bill that day finished a very disappointing thirty-third following engine melt-down on lap thirty-two. As current fans of the sport are aware, Elliott persevered and eventually achieved substantially greater success on the circuit than he did that February day at the "Rock."

Elliott's presence at the track that day was the direct result of a decision made some years before by his dad, George, regarding his three sons, Ernie, Bill, and Dan. It seems that all three boys were quite fond of going fast in their younger years. In time, that need for speed was expressed on the back roads of Dawson County in an assortment of Ford muscle cars. It wasn't long before the boys had gotten into some close calls and had, er, come to the attention of the local constabulary. Rather than see the boys injured in some informal street race, the senior Elliott opted to get them all involved in formal racing. As the owner of the local Ford dealership, he was in an ideal situation to sponsor that pastime. As it worked out, young Bill proved to be the best behind the wheel of a racing car, while Ernie and Dan took more enjoyment from the mechanical work that went into making the car go fast. By pooling their efforts, the groundwork for a natural team was laid.

By 1976, the boys were ready to try their hand at stock car racing's premier series, the Winston Cup. Perhaps it would be most charitable to call that first season an experience builder, for indeed, that is what it was. Bill made eight starts that season both in his dad's No. 9 Ford and Bill Champion's No. 10 Ford. Those outings produced valuable experience, but no top-ten finishes. Truth be told, young Bill's car was often among the first to drop out during a race.

It wasn't until 1979, after the team had picked up a few of Bobby Allison's old Cam 2 Mercurys, that Bill finally brought home a top-five finish. The team made thirteen appearances that season, the first of which came at their "home" track, Atlanta. After making a number of promising runs early in the season (among them a seventh-place finish in the Rebel 500 at Darlington), Elliott drove his No. 9 Mercury to an impressive second place in the Southern 500 behind race winner David Pearson. After the event, Elliott,

Driver Bill Elliott in his office. Craft Photo

Elliott in his 1987–88 #9 Ford Thunderbird which, according to many Ford drivers, was one of the best stock car body styles ever built—and far superior to anything that's been built by Ford since. Craft Photo

Ernie Elliott is the oldest of George Elliott's three redheaded sons. During the mid-eighties, Ernie was engine builder and crew chief for brother Bill's #9 Thunderbirds. Craft Photo

then considered a rising star on the circuit, said in his thick north Georgia drawl, "We're gainin' on our first win. Maybe we'll win next year."

Though that prediction was off by nearly four seasons, win number one for Elliott and the family team finally came in 1983 after auto parts manufacturer Harry Melling signed on as a major sponsor. When NASCAR downsized in 1981, Bill and the team switched back to Fords. Their small, squared-off Thunderbirds were dressed in black, red, and white Melling racing livery that year. Elliott's first winning season began on a promising note when he finished second behind Cale Yarborough in the Daytona 500.

He got another second at Rockingham one month later, and ultimately scored eleven top-five finishes that season. Win number one came for Elliott at the last race of the year, at Riverside. He qualified his "square-bird" tenth that day, then passed Benny Parsons one lap before a rain-mandated yellow flag caused the field to finish under the caution.

In 1984, the team switched to the new rounded-off Thunderbirds that Ford had unveiled the year before. It proved to be an auspicious change. Elliott used that new body style's superior aerodynamics and his brother Ernie's horsepower to score three

Elliott first found success and top-five finishes behind the wheel of a block-long red-and-white Mercury that had been purchased from Roger Penske's CAM 2 team. Here

Elliott leads Bobby Allison and David Pearson who are piloting equally lumbering cars. Craft Collection

Bill Elliott's first NASCAR win came at Riverside in late 1983. His mount that day was a boxy red, white, and black 1982 Thunderbird. Craft Photo

Elliott was the king of superspeedways in 1987. Above, he is shown leading at Talladega that year. Not a surprise considering his #9 Coors Ford set new high-speed marks just about everywhere it ran in 1987. At this particular race, his qualifying speed was 212+ mph. Craft Photo

Elliott visited victory lane eleven times in 1987, including this one in Michigan. Craft Photo

Though no one knew it at the time, Elliott's '87 Thunderbird proved to be the fastest stock car in history. Craft Photo

wins. Win number two was also Elliott's first superspeedway triumph, and came when he finished ahead of Dale Earnhardt's Chevy at Michigan. His next two wins also came on mile-or-more tracks, Charlotte and Rockingham.

Elliott picked up his "Awesome Bill" nickname in 1985 when he won eleven WC events and the Winston Million. His first 1985 win came at the Daytona 500, where he had put his new Coors-sponsored car on the pole with a record-breaking speed of 205.114mph. Elliott won next at Atlanta, another of the tour's high-speed tracks, and backed it up with yet another superspeedway win at Darlington.

Elliott won the pole at Talladega in 1985 at 209.398mph. During the race, a broken oil fitting seemed to put him out of contention, costing him two laps of track time. Incredibly, Elliott charged back onto the track to lap the whole field—twice—under green flag racing conditions, and ultimately win the race. It was a truly awesome performance and one that caused quite a bit of consternation in both the GM camp and NASCAR's front offices. Elliott had humiliated the Chevrolet competition that day, and his stellar performance also exposed NASCAR's beloved and closely regulated myth of

Elliott took a personal role in many of the mechanical tasks that helped his Coors Thunderbird achieve success. Craft Photo

The Elliott operation in the mid-eighties was a family affair. Bill's brother Dan played a large roll behind the
scenes preparing the cars that helped Bill dominate the
circuit. PPG Archives

door handle-to-door handle competitiveness. Elliott
also had wins at Pocono, Michigan, Darlington (his
first Southern 500), and Atlanta that season. Though
he'd won eleven times to Darrell Waltrip's mere
three, the always-puzzling NASCAR points system
relegated Elliott to second in the 1985 season championship.

Elliott won just two races in 1986. Though he
was once again the fastest man at Daytona, a crash
relegated him to a back-marker finish. He upped
the qualifying speed at Talladega to 212.229mph,
but engine failure caused a DNF at that race. He finally won at Michigan and became the king of the
"Irish Hills" in 1986 when he won the second race
there, too.

Though no one knew it at the time, 1987 was
to be the fastest racing season in NASCAR history.
And, due to the restrictor plates the sanctioning
body introduced in 1988 to slow Elliott and other
Ford drivers down, it's likely that the 1987 season
will remain the fastest for all time. Elliott began the
year by blistering Daytona in qualifying with a hot

In 1992, Bill Elliott signed on with Junior Johnson's famed
Ronda, North Carolina-based team. He picked up the
#11 and Budweiser sponsorship in that team change.
Craft Photo

Elliott encountered more than a little bad luck after leaving the family team. This wreck he suffered at Daytona in the 500 is just one example. Craft Photo

lap of 210.364mph to win the pole, and he dominated the race for his second Daytona 500 win. He turned up the wick even farther at Talladega and qualified first with a 212.809mph lap—the fastest in NASCAR history. Engine problems sidelined his car during the race and another young Ford pilot, Davey Allison, snared the win. Elliott was even fast when it was hot, and he upped Talladega's summer race pole mark to 203.827mph before winning the race handily. He rounded out the season with wins at Michigan, Charlotte, Rockingham, and Atlanta to

finish second in the championship again—this time behind Dale Earnhardt.

NASCAR reintroduced the much-hated restrictor plate in 1988 and speeds dropped more than 10mph at both Daytona and Talladega. Elliott won six times that year, including the Southern 500, even though he was no longer the fastest man on the superspeedways. Interestingly, though the NASCAR rules book had slowed him down enough for the rest of the field (read: Chevrolet race cars) to catch up at Daytona and Talladega, Elliott logged enough top-

The boy from Dawsonville returned home in 1995. Teamed once again with his brothers, Elliott campaigned *this family-backed 1995 Thunderbird in 1995.* Craft Collection

There is a boyish, Huck Finn quality about Elliott that has made him one of NASCAR's most popular drivers. PPG Archives

five finishes to win his first Winston Cup championship in 1988.

Since that season Elliott has not regained his 1985–1988 level of success. He continued on with his Dawsonville-based team until 1992, but only won five times in those three seasons. In 1992, he left Ernie, Dan, and the family team for Junior Johnson's No. 11 Ford and posted six more wins during the three years he worked in Ronda, North Carolina (site of Johnson's shop). Today his total number of wins is forty, which ties him with another north Georgia driver named Tim Flock for twelfth on the all-time win list. For the 1995 season, Elliott returned to Dawsonville to re-team with the family effort in a McDonald's-backed Thunderbird.

CHAPTER 5

Bob, Fonty, and Tim Flock

The influence of moonshine whiskey on the development of what we now know as stock car racing can't be disregarded. The great depression of 1929–1933 hit the southland, still reeling from the destruction of the Civil War, with particular ferocity. Without jobs to provide income, many young southern men of that generation turned their attention to other pursuits in order to put food on the family table. When the ill-advised constitutional banning of sale and consumption of spirituous liquors went into effect in 1919, it created an immediate—and thirsty—black market for the white lightning that industrious and self-reliant residents of the Appalachian mountains had been making since the birth of the republic. With demand high, it didn't take long for entrepreneurs to step in and fill the need. In the Atlanta, Georgia, area one of the most successful of such Depression-era "venture capitalists" was a colorful fellow named Peachtree Williams.

Now that fact, by itself, probably would not have had much effect on the earliest days of stock car competition were it not for his trio of nephews: Robert Newman Flock, Truman Fontello Flock, and Julius Timothy Flock. You see, making the incendiary

Bob (left) and Fonty (right) got their start as competition drivers while running shine in Dawson County, Georgia. Sometimes they took baby brother Tim (center) along for the ride. The Daytona Racing Archives

brew folks called white lightning was only part of the process—the easiest part, actually. Getting the product to market was the tough part that often required late-night high-speed runs from the refining plant (read: still) to parched metropolitan customers. That's where the police came in. Realizing that it was a whole lot easier to staunch the flow of moonshine than discover and root out every backwoods still, John Law took to interdicting 'shine shipments with roadblocks and high-pursuit cars. Staying out of jail required staying ahead of the boys in blue. It was a race that required both superior horsepower and driving skills. With Atlanta-area mechanics like Red Vogt providing the ponies, Bob and Fonty Flock quickly developed into two of the most skilled north Georgia 'shine runners, and they introduced baby brother Tim to the "sport" by taking him along shotgun on some of their high-speed nocturnal jaunts.

Of course running 'shine wasn't a five-day-a-week, forty-hour job, so hot-shot drivers like the Flock brothers often had time on their hands. Before long they and other similarly situated young men took to staging informal competitions, just to see who had the fastest car. From such clandestine con-

Fonty, Bob, and Tim Flock (left to right) were three of NASCAR's earliest stars. They are shown here while Bob and Tim were driving for Carl Kiekhaefer's Mercury Outboards team. The Daytona Racing Archives

Fonty Flock often raced in his shorts in the days when NASCAR cars still raced on the beach in Daytona. It was Fonty who scored Chevrolet's first NASCAR win in 1955. The Daytona Racing Archives

Tim Flock was NASCAR Grand National champ during the '55 season. He won the title in Carl Kiekhaefer's Chrysler 300 race cars. The Daytona Racing Archives

frontations the sport of stock car racing was born, and as seasoned 'shine runners, the Flock brothers were some of the series' earliest stars. Bob and Fonty launched their racing careers in the late-1930s, running on dirt tracks around the same Dawsonville, Georgia, (famous more recently for a red-haired fellow named Elliott) area where they ran 'shine for $40 a trip. It wasn't until 1947 that Tim ran his first race, at North Wilkesboro.

When Bill France's fledgling NASCAR organization staged an experimental stock car race at the Broward Speedway in south Florida on February 27, 1949, Bob Flock handily won the event. That five-lap, 10mi affair being deemed a success, four months later NASCAR and France organized the first "Strictly Stock" (the original name for what is now called the Winston Cup division) race in Charlotte, North Carolina. Bob Flock drove a '46 Hudson to the pole position at NASCAR race No. 1 with a 67.958mph lap of the 3/4mi, dirt-track Charlotte Speedway. Fonty and

Tim were also in the field, Fonty behind the wheel of a '49 Hudson and Tim in an Olds '88. Fonty finished second, Tim fifth, and Bob thirty-second (due to engine failure). Bob was the most successful of the trio in that first eight-race season, winning twice and finishing in the top five three other times.

Tim's first NASCAR win came in 1950 at Charlotte when he edged out brother Bob to win the second Grand National event at the venue. Fonty's first win also came in 1950 when he drove an Olds to victory on the always treacherous 1mi circular dirt track in Langhorne, Pennsylvania. History shows that Tim was the most successful driver of the three brothers. In his twelve-year Grand National career, Tim won forty events and two national driving championships (1952 and 1955)—a level of success that still ranks him 12th on the all-time win list (a position he currently shares with another north Georgia driver named Elliott). Fonty, on the other hand, won nineteen GN races, while Bob won four.

HUDSON HORNET 7X ENGINE

The automobile engine which powered the Hudson Hornet of the 1950's was the most powerful 'FlatHead' engine mass produced in modern times. When . . . on Motorcar engineers placed this . . . in the beautiful 'Stepdown' . . . machine was virtually . . . ck . . . circuit . . . version

Tim Flock's earliest NASCAR success came thanks to the incredible torque churned out by the Hudson straight-six flathead motor. Craft Photo

As mentioned, Tim Flock won his first national driver's title in 1952 when he drove a Hudson Hornet for Atlanta car dealer Ted Chester. In NASCAR's early days, dirt tracks were the rule rather than the exception, and Hudsons were the hot car on the circuit. Not because they were the most powerful cars on the track, you understand. Truth be known, their flat-head, straight-six engines were barely capable of churning out 170hp, even when fitted with a twin one-barrel carburetor induction system that had been specially developed for stock car competition. But what a Hudson Hornet lacked in horsepower was made up for in spades by the gobs of low-revving torque their I-6 engines cranked out. That proved to be just the ticket for getting off of a dirt track corner with expedition. Tim won eight times that season and finished in the top five at fourteen more events on his way to the Grand National driving championship. His brother Fonty (who'd finished second in the points chase in 1951) finished fourth in the standings after winning the Southern 500 and one other race.

Though Tim did not win another Grand National Championship in 1953, that season he earned perhaps an even more enduring type of fame. You see, that was the season he went racing with "co-driver" Jocko Flocko, and boy, was Flocko a wild animal. He was a Rhesus monkey, in fact, and quite a dapper one at that since he had his own custom-tailored driver's suit and goggles. The idea of Jocko spending

time on the circuit came from Ted Chester, Flock's team sponsor. The idea was to generate publicity, and did it ever. The media loved it, and so did Flock until late in a race in Raleigh, North Carolina, when Jocko got out of the nylon safety belts that kept him strapped into an elevated seat on the passenger's side of the car. According to Flock, as soon as he got free, Jocko pulled on the trap door lanyard (which allowed Flock to check right front tire wear during the race—a common feature on early GN cars). When the spinning tire hit the little monkey in the head he went berserk. Flock was forced to grab the monkey with one hand and steer for the pits with the other. Flock was leading the race at the time, and the extra pit stop cost him a victory. All told, Jocko Flocko "competed" in about thirteen races with Flock during the 1953 season.

Tim's best year on the circuit was 1955, but it happened almost by chance. The year before he had actually quit in disgust after having his win at Daytona (at the February beach race) taken away by Bill France for a minor technical infraction. Though Flock won the race, a post-event tear-down revealed the inside of his carburetor had been polished, and France took away the victory. Flock was incensed and vowed to never race in NASCAR again.

When 1954 rolled around, Flock was operating a Pure Oil station in Atlanta and had no intention of running in another NASCAR race. In fact, he wasn't even going to attend the Daytona Beach race until a group of his friends persuaded him to go. Arriving in Daytona a few days before the race, he and his buddies were taking in time trials at the track when a Chrysler 300 rocketed by on Daytona's wide, flat beach. Flock recalls saying out loud that if he had a car like that (the Chrysler) he'd surely win the race. Unbeknownst to Flock, a local Mercury Outboard dealer was standing nearby and overheard his remark. Recognizing Flock and recalling that he'd won the race the year before (before being disqualified), the dealer offered to introduce him to Carl Kiekhaefer, the Mercury Marine president who sponsored the Chrysler team that had impressed Flock. As luck would have it, Kiekhaefer was looking for a driver and he hired Flock on the spot. Flock won the pole for the race (with a speed of 91.99mph) and took second behind Fireball Roberts' Fish Carburetor Buick. In a case of turnabout being fair play, Flock and Kiekhaefer learned at breakfast the next day that Roberts' car had been disqualified by France for illegal push rods, and that Flock had been named the winner.

The rest of the season was an incredible success for Flock, who won his second Grand National championship. Kiekhaefer paid Flock a salary of $2,500 per month during the 1955 season and let him keep every penny of prize money he won, too. But he expected a lot in return for his money. Team drivers (at one time Kiekhaefer had six or seven cars on the team) were expected to follow his orders to the letter and had to follow a strict curfew during a race week. They also had to keep close track of what their car's gauges read during time trials and then report on those readings during a debriefing much like those that military pilots went through. According to Flock, Kiekhaefer was a perfectionist and expected to win every race his team entered (and, in fact, they very nearly did).

Though the money was incredible (on top of the salary and prize money, Kiekhaefer often gave Flock a bonus of several hundred dollars when he won), in time Flock grew tired of following Kiekhaefer's orders—especially after Kiekhaefer started telling the team which of its numerous drivers he wanted to win. According to Flock, Kiekhaefer would walk out on the track during a race and flag him in, just to let another of the team's drivers win the race.

"When he walked out to the track with a pit board in his hand, you had to pit or he would fire you," Flock said in an interview. Ultimately, it was these manipulations that caused Flock to quit the team in April 1956. But not before he had won an incredible eighteen races during the 1955 season—the most that any driver had won in a season until that time. (Flock's one-season victory record wasn't broken until Richard Petty's phenomenal success in 1967.) Flock ran in fourteen more races in 1956 after leaving Kiekhaefer, but won only once more (his fortieth and final career victory) at Elkhart Lake in a Bill Stroppe-prepared M335 Mercury.

Though Flock continued to race until 1961, he never again achieved the success of 1952 and 1955. His career came to what was perhaps a premature end in 1961 when Big Bill France banned him from the series for life. When Flock backed Curtis Turner's attempt to unionize the NASCAR drivers, France banned both from the sport. Though Turner was allowed to return in 1966, Flock never again pulled on a racing helmet. All three of the Flock brothers are now members of the National Motorsports Hall of Fame.

Following his departure from Kiekhaefer's team, Tim Flock drove red-and-white M335 Mercurys for California racer Bill Stroppe. Craft Photo

CHAPTER 6

Ray Fox, Sr.

In the world of stock car racing it goes without argument that it is the drivers who receive the most media attention and fan adoration. Mechanics, shop workers, and even the fairly high-profile members of a team's race day pit crew seldom, if ever, get to bask in the warm glow of the public spotlight. But where would a "star" driver be without them? The answer is obvious.

Even though it is the drivers who get the most sports page ink, the history of the Grand National Division (nee Winston Cup) does number among its famed luminaries the names of some team owners and chief mechanics whose skills were such that the whole racing world came to know them. Ray Fox, Sr., is certainly in that category, and cars that Fox wrenched on won 140 races from 1962 to 1974. Though Fox no longer actively campaigns on the circuit, he is still involved in the sport as one of NASCAR's most respected technical inspectors. But perhaps we're getting ahead of ourselves.

To begin at the beginning, Raymond Lee Fox was born in Pelham, New Hampshire, in 1917, far

Ray Fox (left) and Junior Johnson (right) were a perfect combination in NASCAR racing. Fox's mechanical genius coupled with Johnson's daring behind the wheel produced many wins. The Daytona Racing Archives

from the Blue Ridge mountains that nurtured so many of the first stars of stock car racing. At twenty-eight he turned his back on New England and its harsh winters and headed south to Florida, a migration that still takes place today. The Sunshine State to which Fox traveled in 1945 did not boast of Disney World, Sea World—or any other tourist attraction "world" for that matter. But it did feature a wide, dense-packed expanse of silver sand where people interested in automobiles had been coming to set speed records almost since a German fellow named Daimler invented the very first internal combustion engine.

Fox first tried his hand at driving when not working his "day job" at Robert Fish's Daytona carburetor manufacturing company. He also worked on cars Fish sponsored for up-and-coming driver Fireball Roberts. In fact, Roberts and Fox were driving teammates in several early years of Grand National competition. It soon became obvious that Fox's greatest talent was mechanical, not driving, and by the mid-fifties, Fox had hung up his driving gloves for good.

Fox was responsible for maintaining Johnson's Mystery Motor Impalas in 1963. The #3 Impalas that Fox built for Johnson were Chevrolet's last hurrah in NASCAR racing until 1971. Craft Photo

Since the engines Fox built produced bucketsfull of horsepower, his talents as a mechanic were in high demand. In 1955, Fox built the engine for Fireball's beach course Buick, and even though he only started on the engine the evening before the February 27 event (due to the sponsor's last-minute decision to back Roberts in the race), Fireball led every lap of the race and should have scored his first GN beach course win. However, the sanctioning body disqualified his car—twenty-four hours after the fact—for allegedly having push rods that were 16/100in too long.

Fox's first official GN engine-building success came the next year, when he and Herb Thomas worked for Carl Kiekhaefer's dominating Chrysler 300 team. Fox helped drivers Thomas, Buck Baker, and Speedy Thompson win twenty-two of the first twen-

ty-six races they ran in 1956, including an incredible string of sixteen straight victories. Buck Baker won the Grand National championship and teammates Thomas and Thompson finished second and third, respectively. Fox's role in the team's success did not go unnoticed, and he was named NASCAR's 1956 mechanic of the year.

In 1957, Fox opened his own garage in Daytona Beach and started preparing cars and race engines for other teams. Fox-prepared cars soon appeared in victory lanes all across the South. One especially notable victory came in 1960, when Junior Johnson piloted a Chevrolet that Fox built in the week before the Daytona 500 to his first Big D win. Johnson, now a car owner in the Winston Cup ranks, still remembers that victory fondly and calls it the favorite of his fifty GN wins as a driver.

After General Motors finally nailed the back door of its racing divisions in the early sixties, Fox switched mechanical allegiances to Dodge. The Daytona Racing Archives

The Fox and Johnson partnership produced two more wins that season (at South Boston, Virginia, and Hickory, North Carolina), and Chevrolet invited Fox to work on the new Corvair. Rather than preparing the car that Ralph Nader loved to hate for racing, Fox's job was to improve the fuel economy of its rear-mounted, flat-six-cylinder motor. Ultimately, Betty Skelton (aviatrix and sometime NASCAR speed trial driver) won the Pure Oil Economy Run competition that year with a fuel consumption average of 98mph.

Fox worked with Johnson and Chevrolet for the next few years, and also prepared Pontiacs for drivers like Jim Paschal and David Pearson. In fact, it was a Fox-prepped '61 Pontiac that a youthful David Pearson drove to his first Grand National victory at the 1961 World 600, a win that was a major surprise in several ways. For one thing, Fox's Pontiac was officially without a driver until just one week before the grueling 600mi race at Charlotte. And Pearson, still in his pre-"Silver Fox" days, was just a fresh-faced kid from Spartanburg in one of his first races on the circuit. The odds didn't favor a Pearson victory, yet Pearson and Fox's Pontiac ended up in victory lane

while the cars of series stars like Fireball Roberts, Joe Weatherly, and Rex White were either in the garage area or wadded into big balls of scrap metal.

The year of the Chevrolet "Mystery Motor" was 1963and it was Fox who played a major role in making these all-new, race-only engines perform under extremely difficult conditions. "Big Three" interest in Grand National victories had increased exponentially since the inception of the series. By the early sixties the rivalry between the automakers had grown to the point that whole catalogs full of special "off highway" or "police package" parts were being produced solely for NASCAR cars. As long as these parts were at least ostensibly available to the general public, NASCAR officials were not inclined to make a stink about their nonstock nature. As you might have guessed, things ultimately got out of control. By 1962, for example, Pontiac offered an over-the-counter 421ci "Super Duty" engine package that helped Fireball Roberts' Catalina run like the dickens on the track. The only rub was, it never came factory installed in any regular production car, and unless your name was Yunick or Fox, you had very little chance of actually buying one from your local dealer.

When Fast Freddie Lorenzen attempted a comeback in 1970 (following his 1967 retirement), Fox provided a winged Daytona for him to run. The Daytona Racing Archives

Taking a page from Pontiac's book for 1963, Chevrolet engineers cooked up an all-new, stagger-valved big-block engine that had few if any components in common with the 409 engines powering street-going Impalas. And man, was that engine fast—especially with a master mechanic like Ray Fox turning the wrenches. Built in only limited numbers (according to Smokey Yunick, fewer than forty-eight of the 427 engines were ever cast) and kept a closely guarded secret, the new power plants quickly came to be called Mystery Motors. Their ability to propel a '63 Impala around a racetrack was no secret once Speed Weeks 1963 rolled around. Junior Johnson scorched the NASCAR record book with his new Fox-prepared No. 3 Chevy in qualifying. The fastest speed recorded at Daytona in 1962 had been just over 152mph. Johnson's 1963 qualifying run made him the fastest man in NASCAR racing with a new track record of 165.183mph. Non-Chevrolet teams raised a hue and cry about the new Mystery Motor's non-"stock" nature even before Johnson's new car had cooled down from its record-shattering run.

Though teething trouble ultimately sidelined Johnson's 427 during the race (push rods broke with

The motors that Fox prepared for Johnson's '63 Impalas were a mystery to most non-Chevrolet outsiders. Built in only limited numbers specifically for racing, they were the forerunners of the modern Chevy "Rat" motor. Craft Photo

Though in his eighties, Ray Fox is still a vital and active part of NASCAR racing. One of NASCAR's outstanding car owners and crew chiefs, Fox now keeps contemporary car owners and crew chiefs in line as a NASCAR inspector. Craft Collection

regularity), Chevrolet execs, already worried about an antitrust action by the federal government (GM was the biggest automaker in the world in those days), ultimately got cold feet about the new engine and ceased its production. Adding insult to injury, they even tried to "repossess" the few engines that had made it into racing circulation. Johnson and Fox were able to keep the few engines they had but were firmly told that no replacement parts would be forthcoming. Finishing out the season was a real challenge, and in a strange twist of fate, Fox and Johnson actually had to buy back a Mystery Motor from Ford's Holman and Moody racing "factory," which bought it for evaluation earlier in the year. Though crippled by the lack of parts and factory support, Johnson and Fox were still able to win seven races that year (including the Dixie 400 and the National 400), sit on the pole at several more, and literally pack the grandstands with Chevrolet fans.

After the 1963 season, Johnson parked his Mystery Motor-equipped Impala for good, and along with Fox, switched to Dodge. The two found almost immediate success with the new mechanical combination (Johnson won a 100mi qualifier during Speed Weeks 1964 and finished ninth in the 500). Even so, by April, Johnson had switched to Ford.

Fox, on the other hand, remained associated with Chryco for most of the balance of his racing career. The 426 Hemi-powered race cars he prepared were driven by many of the era's best Grand National drivers. Buck Baker, for example, won the 1964 Southern 500 in a Fox-prepared Dodge. Three years later, Buck's son Buddy got his first GN victory in another Fox-built Dodge at the 1967 National 500 at Charlotte. In 1968, the younger Baker won the World 600 at Charlotte in a new, fuselage-bodied, Fox-prepared Charger.

When the Aero-Wars erupted in 1969, Ray Fox fielded slippery new Dodge Charger 500s and, later, their radically winged replacements, Dodge Charger Daytonas. Those "day-glo" red No. 6 Dodges were often the fastest cars on the track.

By the seventies, Fox was losing his enthusiasm for racing. With factory support on the wane and fabrication costs on the rise, he retired from racing in 1972 and opened a tire dealership in Daytona Beach. Recently, Fox has returned to racing as a NASCAR technical inspector. Having one of the greatest stock car mechanics of all time in charge of inspecting Winston Cup cars is no doubt an effective way to keep the current crop of crew chiefs in close conformance with the modern NASCAR rules book.

CHAPTER 7

Bill France, Sr

William Henry Getty France was born just outside of Washington, D.C., on September 26, 1909. Born a strapping baby, he grew in stature to be a big man. Both his 6ft 4in stature coupled with ambitions that were equally Homeric in size earned him the nickname "Big" Bill at an early age. While in high school, France played varsity basketball and worked after school repairing cars at service stations and a local Ford dealership. It is perhaps that early exposure to things mechanical that charted the course Big Bill would follow in life.

After developing an interest in motor racing, France began to spend time as a fan at local races, and at the age of seventeen he raced his own car for the first time. He continued racing on D.C.-area dirt tracks even after meeting and marrying his wife, Anne, in 1931. France worked during the day to support his soon growing family, but the evenings and weekends he spent working on and racing cars that he had built.

France moved south in 1934, heading for Miami. The relocation was anything but well-funded. At

Bill France was a big man with bigger ideas. They led directly to the National Association for Stock Car Auto Racing. The Daytona Racing Archives

the time, the France family had the grand sum of $75 in a Washington bank account and $25 in cash to fund the trip. They also had Big Bill's mechanic's tools, with which he hoped to underwrite the trip by performing repair work along the way. When the France caravan got to Daytona, the racer in Big Bill forced a stop just to see the world famous beach where so many drivers had come to set new land speed records. After a look around the town and a dip in the ocean, Bill and Anne decided they had come far enough south and thoughts of Miami receded with the tide.

France quickly found auto-related work and put the family up in rented accommodations. In time, France opened up his own service station on Daytona's main street and the family prospered. His arrival in Daytona couldn't have come at a better time for the city fathers. When Sir Malcolm Campbell and others decided to move their land speed records to the Bonneville Salt Flats in Utah, Daytona officials, aware of the tourist value that high-speed beach events afforded, set up the first organized races on the beach. At first, France was simply

Bill France cut a dapper figure in the fifties and did much to convince automakers and the general public that stock car racing was a legitimate sport. Craft Collection

fied automobiles of American manufacture. The premier division was to be called "Strictly Stock," and cars that competed in this class were only allowed a handful of modifications away from stock in the name of increased safety.

The idea was to attract the general motoring public by featuring cars just like the ones they drove every day of the week. As history attests, it was an idea with a spark of genius that eventually grew into the most popular form of motorsports in the nation. The first strictly stock race was held in June 1949 at a dirt track just outside of Charlotte, North Carolina. It attracted a crowd of 13,000 paying spectators and a field of thirty-three cars. Nine different manufacturers were represented on the starting grid and many of the drivers who took the green flag that day ultimately wound up as inductees in the National Motorsports Press Association's Hall of Fame. Curtis Turner, Tim, Bob, and Fonty—the Flock brothers, Red Byron, Lee Petty, and Herb Thomas were all in Charlotte that day and all later became stars of the fledgling NASCAR series. Also in the field of that very first NASCAR race was a woman named Sara Christian and the eventual race winner, Jim Roper, who had towed his Lincoln all the way from Great Bend, Kansas.

The race was scheduled to last 150mi and the attrition rate was high. By race's end, wrecks and mechanical failures had claimed all but five cars that remained running. Lee Petty, driving a Buick borrowed from a friend, was the victim of NASCAR's first (and the race's only) wreck, leaving the Buick much the worse for wear on the return trip home. Glenn Dunnaway was the victim of another kind of first that day, too: the NASCAR rules book. Though flagged the winner of the event, a postrace inspection revealed that his former (perhaps current) moonshine car had been fitted with reinforced rear springs, disqualifying it from strictly stock status. Dunnaway was DQ'd by the sanctioning body and ultimately took NASCAR to court—where his case was thrown out. The National Association for Stock Car Automobile Racing had gotten off to a successful start.

The series grew, and the yearly beach race at Daytona soon became one of the premier events on the schedule. Held each February, the race consisted of thirty-nine laps (160mi) around a 4.1mi course laid out over portions of the sandy beach and an adjacent section of paved U.S. Highway A1A. When the Darlington Superspeedway was opened in 1950, the Southern 500 held there in the fall immediately became a prestigious event to win. Oval-shaped with one set of corners smaller that the other, Darlington was a challenging track to drive and quickly became the second fastest venue (after Daytona) on the circuit.

Other men might have been satisfied with the circuit's early success, but Bill France was a dreamer who was convinced that stock car racing would be-

one of many competitors who took part in those events. Later, when city officials decided that the races were a losing venture, France stepped in to take over their promotion. The rest, as they say, is history.

In 1947, France called a meeting of drivers, mechanics, and promoters who had been participating in the growing sport of stock car racing. Those in attendance met in Daytona's old Ebony Lounge to discuss the possibility of forming a national sanctioning body for the sport. One of the thirty-five men in attendance was legendary mechanic and race driver Louis Jerome "Red" Vogt, who owned a garage in Atlanta. Vogt had been a next-door neighbor to the France family in D.C. before Bill was born. It was Vogt, according to most accounts, who came up with the NASCAR name for France's new organization, and news reports about the meeting were the first time the racing world heard about the National Association for Stock Car Automobile Racing.

The original plan, as decided upon that day, was to establish a racing series for modified and unmodi-

come a truly national sport with the right supervision. Noting Darlington's success as a race venue, France began making plans for his own superspeedway, only the track that France envisioned would be far larger and permit much faster lap speeds. High-speed, door-to-door competition was what the buying public wanted, and France intended to supply that demand in spades.

France completed the construction of his vision on a tract of swampy ground just west of downtown Daytona Beach in 1958. Rather than being configured as a traditional oval, France's new track featured four turns, a long back stretch and a tri-oval section that, when viewed from the stands, seemed to point onrushing cars directly at the spectators seated there. And, oh yes, the turns were steeply banked. Enough dirt was quarried from the infield, in fact, to bank the four-lane racing surface at a difficult-to-climb 33 degrees. In short, the new 2.5mi-long track was built to be a palace of speed. And it was.

Cotton Owens ran better than 143mph in qualifying for the inaugural Daytona 500—a speed more than 40mph faster than the fastest hot laps on the old beach course or at Darlington. Some 41,921 fans crowded into the speedway to watch the first race on February 22, 1959. Fifty-nine Grand National cars took the green flag that day and over the course of the race the lead changed no fewer than thirty-three times. When the event's 200 laps had been run, it took race officials sixty-one hours of examining photos of the finish before they were able to officially determine that Lee Petty's Oldsmobile had just edged out Johnny Beauchamp's Thunderbird for the win. Door-to-door racing at break-neck speed was what France had wanted and that's exactly what he got. The fans loved it, too.

As NASCAR grew, so, too, did France's power over the sport. It's not unfair to say that Big Bill ruled with an iron hand and was unwilling to brook any questioning of his authority. In NASCAR, things were

The house that France built. Opened in 1959, the Daytona International Speedway quickly became one of the premier racing circuits in the world. The Daytona Racing Archives

France ruled his kingdom with a strong hand. He wasn't above backing up his decisions with force. In 1961, he took a gun to a meeting where drivers were trying to organize. Here he is in 1969 "disproving" the unsafe track conditions at Talladega by turning hot laps in a Ford he bought from Holman and Moody. *The Daytona Racing Archives*

France's son, Bill "Jr.", carries on his father's control of NASCAR today. *Craft Photo*

done for "the good of racing," and it was France who ultimately decided just exactly what that "good" was to be. But perhaps that's exactly what was needed to coalesce the disorganized and unsanctioned bull ring dirt track races of the late forties into a truly national sport. Even France's detractors—and he collected more than a few—can't deny that by sheer force of will he was able to create what has become today the most popular form of motorsports competition in the country. France's International Speedway Corporation eventually built another, even-faster superspeedway in Talladega, Alabama, purchased fabled Darlington Raceway, and bought a major interest in the equally historic road course in Watkins Glen, New York. Mr. France presided over his empire until shortly before his death in June 1992. He was eighty-two years old. Today his son William Clifton France (Bill, Jr.) runs the stock car racing empire that his father first put together back in 1947.

Junior Johnson

Robert "Junior" Johnson has been called the "last American hero." While the "last" appellation might be suspect, there is little doubt about his hero status. According to racing lore, Johnson, a native of Wilkes County, North Carolina, stepped out from behind a mule and into stock car racing. While still fond of plowing his Ronda, North Carolina, garden with mule power, Johnson didn't actually put down the reins and slide behind the wheel of a Grand National race car. Though that transition came in time, Junior went to stock car preparatory school first.

He ran moonshine.

The making of moonshine—white lightning, Mountain Dew, or just plain old home brew whiskey—wasn't considered a crime during the gritty days of the Depression as much as it was simply seen as the exercise of an individual's right to survive. Heck, folks in the Appalachians had been making moonshine ever since the earliest days of the republic, and in the prohibition years that skill once again became the best way to convert a corn crop into cash. Even after prohibition had been repealed, it still made dollars and sense to make moonshine because it wasn't taxed by the federal government. As a result, a drinking man's dollar went a whole lot farther with home brew than a store-bought brand.

The only trouble for the industry was the distance between its city consumers and the rural stills that were stoked to life nearly every night. Enter fearless young men like Junior Johnson who had an uncanny ability to keep their hopped-up 'shine cars one step ahead of the revenue agents who were often in hot pursuit. Though the risks of that nocturnal avocation were high (death in a fiery crash or an extended jail sentence if caught), the rewards were equally high, and a 'shine driver could pocket $40 to $50 for every run he made. Two or three runs a week resulted in a monthly income of more than $600—all the money in the world in the rural South during the Depression. And that's just when (in 1931) and where Robert "Junior" Johnson was born. More particularly, in Wilkes County, North Carolina, which in 1935 had been the site of the largest single seizure of moonshine in history. Perhaps it was inevitable then that Johnson would become a 'shine driver and eventually one of the greatest drivers in NASCAR his-

Today Junior Johnson ranks as one of the winningest drivers and team owners in NASCAR history. Craft Photo

Junior Johnson got his start as a 'shine runner in Ronda, North Carolina. By the sixties, he was a bona fide star on the NASCAR tour. The Daytona Racing Archives

This was Johnson's office during the season he campaigned mystery motor Impalas. Craft Photo

tory. As mentioned, Johnson ran 'shine for a number of years before entering his first stock car event. He even served time in jail after failing to foil the revenuers on one particular occasion. To Junior's driving credit, it wasn't a defect in his skill behind the wheel that resulted in his arrest. Instead, it was a sneaky revenue agent lying in wait who caught Junior one morning while he was firing his father's still.

Junior's first taste of competitive driving came at the suggestion of his brother L.C. in the late-1950s. Junior was plowing in the garden one day when L.C. asked him if he'd like to drive L.C.'s car in a modified race that Saturday at nearby North Wilkesboro Speedway (which is still one of the toughest short tracks on the circuit today). Johnson figured it would be more fun than looking at the southern end of his mule, so he agreed. He won the race and went on to become a force on the modified circuit.

His first Grand National start came in 1953 at the Southern 500 in Darlington. Johnson drove a No. 75

Olds Holiday and qualified twenty-sixth. A crash down the back stretch at the Lady in Black on lap 222 brought his first GN outing to a premature conclusion. Though he was forced to watch Buck Baker go on to win the 500 that day, Darlington's victory lane would soon host Johnson's car as well as those belonging to his team's drivers.

Johnson's first Grand National win came in 1953 at Hickory, where he finished ahead of Tim Flock—ultimately that year's national champ—in a 100mi dirt track event. Johnson campaigned a No. 55 Olds that day and pocketed a winner's purse of $1,000. Race accounts referred to Junior as "the lead foot driver with the large belly," and Johnson would lose neither

his ample midriff nor his heavy right foot during the following eleven years of his driving career. At the close of the '55 season, Johnson had won five times and was ranked sixth in championship points. Six more wins followed in 1958 as Johnson drove a No. 11 '57 Ford. Johnson piloted the same car to five more wins in 1959 before switching to Chevrolet for his first superspeedway triumph.

As the 1960 racing season started, Junior was without a regular ride. Legendary mechanic Ray Fox was also between teams and undecided about entering a car in the upcoming Daytona 500, even though he lived just across town from the track. Just a week or so before the race, some backers with Day-

When GM got out of racing Johnson switched to Ford's "Going Thing." At first he drove his own team Galaxies. Later he prepared cars for other drivers. One of the most successful of those was LeeRoy Yarbrough. In 1969, LeeRoy and Junior won just about everything on the circuit. Craft Collection

In 1969, Junior Johnson prepared slippery Torino Talladegas and Cyclone Spoiler IIs for LeeRoy Yarbrough. They began the season with a win in the Daytona 500 and won just about every superspeedway race over the rest of the season. Craft Collection

When Ford decided to abandon NASCAR racing in 1971, Johnson switched back to Chevrolet. He, Robert Yates, and Bobby Allison made that marque a power on the circuit again and scored the first wins for the new Monte Carlo body style. The Daytona Racing Archives

Recently, Johnson has returned to Ford. His cars are often the fastest on the track. Here his two team Thunderbirds captured both the inside and outside pole positions for the Daytona 500. Craft Photo

tona Beach Kennel Club sponsorship approached Fox about preparing a '59 Chevy for the 500. Though he thought the project was hopeless, Fox signed on anyway. Twenty-hour work days filled with wrenching on the No. 27 Chevy ensued, and the car was finished just in time for newly signed driver Junior Johnson to qualify it ninth. During the race, Johnson, described by the local paper as "the well fed mountain kid from Ronda, North Carolina," took advantage of a late race spin by Bobby Johns to win the race in storybook fashion. Johnson drove Kennel Club-sponsored Chevrolets to two more wins that season and at times also drove Fords for the Woods Brothers' team. In 1961, Junior switched to Pontiacs and picked up his now famous Holly Farms sponsorship for the first time. The cars he drove to seven GN victories that year all raced under No. 27. He stayed with Pontiacs in '62 and joined up with Ray Fox again in the National 500 in Charlotte to take his second superspeedway win in Fox's No. 3 car.

During the off-season, Fox and Johnson were invited to a test session of Pontiac cars and Chevrolets powered by a mysterious new big-block engine developed just for racing. Built around a beefy four-bolt main-journaled block and free-flowing stagger-valved heads, the new 427 looked like a winner and ran like one, too. Fox and Johnson were convinced and quickly decided to campaign new Impalas for '63. Things were going well with their preparations until just before the beginning of the season when, according to Johnson, Chevy management attempted to shut down all "Mystery Motor" operations. They even tried to take back the handful of motors that had already been provided. Ultimately, Fox and Johnson persuaded Chevrolet otherwise. Even so, they were told in no uncertain terms that the engines and spares on hand would be the only parts provided to the team for the rest of the season.

When Ford drivers got wind of the all-new racing engine they were understandably upset by its non-production nature (in fact, Chevrolet would never build even one production car with a 427 Mystery Motor for power), and raised quite a fuss. Chevrolet, in an attempt to quell the Ford protests, was forced to sell one of the precious engines to John Holman (of the Ford-based Holman and Moody team) when he attempted to call Chevrolet's bluff about the engine's over-the-counter availability.

Johnson and Fox showed up at Daytona with their new No. 3 Impala ready to test the car against the rest of the 1963 500 field. They collectively flunked that exam when Johnson streaked around the Big D at a record shattering qualifying speed of 165.183mph to clinch the pole for the race. He also convincingly won one of the 500's two qualifying races. Unfortunately, the new Mystery Motor's lack of R&D time caught up with it during the race and Johnson fell out with engine trouble on lap twenty-six. That was basically the story for Johnson and Fox for the balance of the season. Though their Mystery Motor cars were lightning fast in qualifying, they often broke well before the finish. And with spare parts in short supply, that got to be an increasingly bigger problem as the season progressed. Eventually, Fox was forced to buy back the Mystery Motor that Chevrolet had sold to Holman and Moody just so the team could complete the season. And what a strange turn of events that was: the leading Chevrolet mechanic showing up at the Holman and Moody Ford race "factory" parts counter looking for replacement parts!

Johnson and Fox eventually won seven races in 1963 with their Mystery Motor cars—including superspeedway events at Atlanta and Charlotte—and the team was wildly popular with the fans (if not the Ford and Chryco competition). With no more parts being forthcoming, Johnson and Fox shut down the Mystery Motor team for '64 and, after a brief stint as Fox's '64 Dodge driver, Johnson decided to get with the Ford program. For the next two years he drove Galaxies for Banjo Matthews ('64) and for himself ('65 and '66), earning the balance of his fifty Grand National wins. Today Johnson is currently ranked eighth on NASCAR's all-time win list along with Ned Jarrett.

Johnson's last race as a driver came at Rockingham in the 1966 American 500. But it was far from the end of his NASCAR career. When the tour returned to Daytona in 1967, so did Johnson, this time as team owner for the Fairlane driven by Darel Dieringer in the 500. In fact, Johnson had already made one foray as a car owner in 1966 when, at Atlanta, he fielded an independent Galaxie (during the Ford boycott that year) for Fred Lorenzen. In so do-

Sterling Marlin drove for Johnson and Maxwell House in the early nineties. Craft Photo

Johnson also provided cars for Geoff Bodine and Bill Elliott with Budweiser backing. Craft Photo

ing he added yet another colorful page to the NASCAR record book. As noted, Ford was in self-imposed exile for most of the '66 season due to a dispute with Bill France about the legality of the 427 single overhead cam motor for GN competition. By the middle of the season, France and the sanctioning body said they would look favorably upon any independent Ford teams that showed up to race, and that's just what Johnson did at Atlanta. But before heading to Georgia, Johnson consulted some of Ford's GT-40 engineers to find out the best way to clean up a '66 Galaxie's boxy aerodynamics. The end result was a yellow race car with such creatively configured sheet metal that folks in the garage area took to calling it the Yellow Banana. In an effort to make the car as aerodynamic as possible Johnson had cut the roll cage and dropped the front of the roof several inches. He had also taken several inches out of the front clip and the Galaxie's hood plunged toward the asphalt at an angle that was far from stock. In another bit of wind management, Johnson also jacked the car's entire rear clip up to the point that it nearly pointed skyward. Though obviously (to the naked eye!) far from any pretense of being stock, NASCAR was so desperate for Ford entries of any kind that they let the car run. Unfortunately for Johnson, his driver that day, Fred Lorenzen, put the car into the

wall. But not before it had led a number of laps. NASCAR did *not* let the Banana car run again.

Dieringer earned Johnson his first GN win as a team owner when he won the Gwyn Staley 400 in North Wilkesboro, just a few miles from Johnson's home. In 1968, Johnson signed LeeRoy Yarbrough as a team driver and switched from Ford to Mercury cars. Their three-year association stretched over the seasons of the factory "Aero-wars" and proved to be a phenomenal success. In 1968, the Grand National circuit became the LeeRoy and Cale (Yarborough) show as those two similarly named (but unrelated) Mercury drivers won nearly every superspeedway race. LeeRoy dominated the big tracks for Johnson in 1969 and became the first NASCAR driver to ever register a "Grand Slam," winning on each of the South's five superspeedways in a single season when he piloted his No. 98 Talladegas and Mercury Spoiler IIs to seven victories.

LeeRoy's record-shattering performance that year earned him more than $187,000, the most money ever won by a NASCAR driver in a single season. The first win for Johnson and his Jacksonville, Florida, driver came at Daytona, where Yarbrough won the 500. Power for that victory came from a 427 Tunnel Port engine built (at Johnson's request) by a Holman and Moody mechanic named Robert

Yates just the day before the race. It would not be the last time that Yates (owner of the No. 28 Ernie Irvan Havoline Ford team) and Johnson would combine efforts to win races.

LeeRoy then drove a Spoiler II to victory in the Rebel 400 at Darlington, and the same car won the World 600 just fifteen days later. By the Firecracker,

Yarbrough was back in a Talladega and he made it two-for-two at Daytona in 1969. They also won that season at Atlanta and at Darlington in the Southern 500.

Though hobbled by Ford's decision to cut back on factory-backed racing activities in 1970, Johnson and Yarbrough still managed to pull off a Spoiler II win at the National 500 in Charlotte.

After that season, Johnson joined with Richard Howard to campaign Chevrolet's new Monte Carlo. Robert Yates, fresh from Holman and Moody, was the team's engine builder and Herb Nab continued on as crew chief. Charlie Glotzbach drove the white No. 3 Chevrolet (painted in the same colors as Johnson's Mystery Motored Impala) in 1971, and the team tasted its first victory at Bristol in the Volunteer 500. That win marked the return of Chevrolet to prominence in the NASCAR circuit. Even more success was waiting in 1972 when Bobby Allison signed on and brought his Coca-Cola sponsorship with him. He and Junior won nine races that first year the series became the Winston Cup circuit.

When Bobby A. departed in 1973, Cale Yarborough signed on as his replacement and over the next eight seasons Johnson and Yarborough were nearly unbeatable. They won fifty-five times and won the Winston Cup championship three years running, from 1976 through 1978.

Darrell Waltrip signed with Johnson in 1981 and the team switched to Buick bodies (retaining corporate Chevrolet power). Johnson won a fourth WC championship that year with the No. 11 Mountain Dew car. DW followed that performance with an identical twelve wins in 1982 and his second straight WC crown. Before parting with Johnson, DW scored nineteen more wins and yet another championship (in 1985 for Chevrolet).

In 1987, Johnson signed on with Ford, which was once again interested in racing. Since then, drivers Terry Labonte, Geoff Bodine, Bill Elliott and Jimmy Spencer have brought Johnson-prepared Thunderbirds home in front thirteen more times.

Johnson's record as a team owner is unmatched. And since he remains active in that capacity on the circuit, that record is sure to improve. It's unlikely that Junior Johnson will have to go back to mule plowing anytime soon.

Johnson takes an active role in the team. He's shown above in action at Charlotte Motor Speedway. Craft Photo

CHAPTER 9

Alan Kulwicki

In many ways, Frank Sinatra's classic song, "My Way," sounds as if it were written about Alan Kulwicki. Born in Wisconsin, far from Winston Cup racing's traditional stomping grounds, and having foregone years of early racing "education" in favor of a B.S. in mechanical engineering (received in 1977 from the University of Wisconsin–Milwaukee), Kulwicki was perhaps the antithesis of the traditional stock car racing driver. Nonetheless, racing was his passion and he set his sights on making a name for himself in NASCAR circles early on.

Born into a family with racing roots—his father had built racing engines for Mario Rossi's Mopar race cars in the sixties and seventies—Kulwicki began his own racing career at an early age. He successfully mixed part-time racing with his school work while growing up in the Milwaukee area, for example. And receipt of his engineering degree coincided with his first career track championship at the Slinger Speedway.

After matriculation, he continued to mix work in the engineering field with midwestern short track racing. Before opting to pursue racing full time, for example, Kulwicki was responsible for developing

Alan Kulwicki had little more than a dream to base his NASCAR plans on in 1985, but he stuck it out to become Winston Cup Champion. Craft Photo

the Indy car alignment system that is still in use today at the Brickyard. Ultimately it became apparent that he would have to choose one activity over the other to achieve the success he knew he was capable of. In 1985, he decided to head south to Winston Cup country and try his luck on the NASCAR tour. He brought with him little more than a car towing a trailer in which to live, and a plan. That plan was to run for Rookie of the Year honors in 1986, run competitively at every track on the circuit in 1987, and win his first NASCAR race in 1988.

He made his first foray into Winston Cup racing that same year and made five racing starts. Race one came at Richmond in September, where he qualified his No. 32 Bill Terry Ford twenty-fifth and brought it home nineteenth, eight laps in arrears of Darrell Waltrip's winning Monte Carlo. His other starts in 1985 came at Dover, Charlotte, Rockingham, and Atlanta. At the end of that season Kulwicki had completed 89 percent of all laps run in the races he had entered and won $10,290 in prize money. Things would get better for Kulwicki's independent operation soon.

Though he'd raced a variety of marques during his short track days, "Special K" campaigned Ford products for all of his Winston Cup career. Craft Photo

In accordance with his plan, Kulwicki ran for the rookie title in 1986. To say that effort was made on a shoestring is not just hyperbole. The fact of the matter is that Kulwicki had but one car, two engines, and two crew members with which to win the title. Yet, incredibly, that's just what he did. His first outing in the car he nicknamed "Sirloin" came at Rockingham. He started twenty-seventh and came home in fifteenth. All told, Kulwicki and his three-man team made twenty-one more starts that season, and during that run, they finished as high as fourth (at Martinsville). When the season was over, Kulwicki's black-and-yellow Quincy's Steak House-sponsored Thunderbird (hence the nickname Sirloin) had made Kulwicki the series' Rookie of the Year. But, of course, that was part of Kulwicki's plan.

Part two of that plan was to be competitive at all tracks on the circuit in 1987 and the Zerex sponsorship that Kulwicki picked up that season helped make that goal a reality. Kulwicki's first pole came at Richmond and he backed up that stellar qualifying performance with two more first-place starts that year.

Kulwicki was one of the drivers who helped Ford race into the future during the early nineties. His #7 Zerex cars were often the fastest during qualifying. Craft Collection

When Zerex withdrew from racing, Kulwicki initially had a tough time securing new sponsorship. Winston provided a one race package for the Daytona 500 that year and

"Special K" campaigned Army Desert Storm colors. Craft Photo

Hooters signed on late in '92 and Kulwicki's championship winning '92 Thunderbird wore white and orange,

Hooter's colors, while leading the pack. Craft Photo

Kulwicki took great pride in his qualifying runs and ultimately proved to be one of the most consistent qualifiers on the circuit.

He made twenty-nine NASCAR starts in 1987 and finished in the top ten at nine of those events. His best run came at Pocono in the Summer 500 where he started second and went on to duke it out with Dale Earnhardt for the win. Chances are that Kulwicki would have prevailed that day if not for one of Earnhardt's patented fender-rubbing spin-out attempts that destabilized Kulwicki's No. 7 T-Bird long enough for Earnhardt to slip past for the victory. Kulwicki's sophomore year on the circuit produced $369,889 in prize money and fifteenth place in the points chase.

Kulwicki's first win came in 1988—right on schedule. He ran twenty-nine races that season, and his best other finishes were a second in the spring Darlington race (formerly the Rebel 500) and at Martinsville. He also came home in the top five at four other venues before he took his first trip to victory lane at Phoenix. Though only qualifying twenty-first

that day, Kulwicki persevered to outdistance Terry Labonte and Davey Allison for the win. Immediately following the checkered flag, Kulwicki spun his car around on the racing surface and took his now-famous "Polish" victory lap. He later said, "That victory lap was something I'd thought about for a long time. I wanted to do something special. There will never be another first win and I wanted to give them something to remember me by." And remember him they did. Kulwicki had eight more top-ten finishes to end up fourteenth in the 1988 championship race.

Nineteen hundred and eighty-nine was a difficult year for his Concord, North Carolina-based team, and though Kulwicki's red, white, and blue Ford had started first at Charlotte, Bristol, Darlington, Rockingham, and Atlanta, he was unable to translate those pole positions into victory. It was during this season that Junior Johnson first approached Kulwicki about signing on as a team driver for one of his Thunderbird-based race car operations. That offer came at Watkins Glen late in the 1989 season and, incredibly, Kulwicki turned it down. Few could believe that Kul-

Kulwicki's racing budget was a shoestring affair during the early years. In '85, he had but one car and two engines, for example. Even when he picked up Zerex spon- *sorship he still had a frugally sized team. This picture shows just about every one of his team's cars, for example.* Craft Photo

wicki had refused Johnson's offer, especially after the difficult year he had in 1989. Of his decision Kulwicki later said, "Time will tell if my decision is right or wrong. But I have never been a quitter in my life. Even as bad as things have been lately, if I joined another team, I would feel like I never stuck it out with what I have now. Down the road I would never be able to say that I have given it my best shot. I would always second-guess myself."

Kulwicki's decision proved to be the right one and at Rockingham in October 1990, he scored his second career WC win. Unfortunately, that victory was dampened somewhat by the announcement that his corporate sponsor, Zerex, would be departing at season's end. Kulwicki was eighth that season in the championship standings with his victory at the "Rock" and twelve other top-ten finishes. Even so, finding a new sponsor was difficult. When Speed Weeks 1991 rolled around, Kulwicki was still sponsorless as he pulled into Daytona with a plain white Thunderbird, unsure of what would happen next.

And that's about when Junior Johnson approached Kulwicki a second time about driving for one of his Ford teams. Incredibly, Kulwicki *again* refused Johnson's offer of a multiyear contract. Luckily, Winston stepped in with sponsorship money for Kulwicki in the 500 and when the green flag fell, his No. 7 Thunderbird sported a Desert Storm-themed Army camouflage paint scheme. He finished eighth in the race and later in the season picked up sponsorship from the bountifully endowed Hooters restaurant chain. By August he was back in victory lane, this time at Bristol, where he outpaced Sterling Marlin (the driver Junior Johnson turned to when Kulwicki refused his second overture). He finished in the top ten another ten more times that year to wind up thirteenth in the championship points race.

Nineteen hundred and ninety-two was the year that Kulwicki's single-minded determination to race only for himself paid off in spades. Once again backed by Hooters, Kulwicki finished fourth in the Daytona 500 that year in a performance suggesting how well the team would ultimately display that season. Kulwicki's car was in victory lane by the sixth race, at Bristol, and he made up for his loss to Earnhardt at Pocono with a victory in the 1992 Championship Spark Plug 500 in June. "Special K" (a nickname Kulwicki picked up in his short track days) turned in fifteen more top ten finishes in 1992 on his way to the Winston Cup Championship, which he clinched with a second-place finish at the season finale in Atlanta. Kulwicki celebrated with another

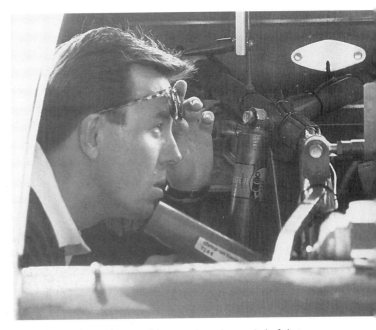

Kulwicki was equal parts driver and engineer. It is fair to say that he could perform just about every mechanical task necessary to campaign his race car by himself. Craft Photo

"Polish" victory lap and the crowd loved it. Though faced with seemingly insurmountable difficulties and imposing odds, Alan Kulwicki had achieved his dream. In just eight short seasons on the circuit, he'd become NASCAR's number-one driver. And he'd done it all on his own. Kulwicki proved to be a humble champion. Upon climbing out of his car in Atlanta he said "I thank God for the fortune to be here and to be an American and compete on the Winston Cup circuit." He went on to reflect, "If you were to bet money back in '86 that I'd be where I am today, the odds were slim. When you consider everything it took to get here from there, you'd say it couldn't be done. But you can't look at it that way. I didn't. Obstacles are what you see when you take your eyes off the goal."

Incredibly, unbelievably, and tragically, Kulwicki would be given very little time to savor his 1992 championship. While returning from a promotional event in April 1993, the plane in which he was riding crashed on final approach to the airport at Bristol, Tennessee. NASCAR's reigning champion was just thirty-nine at the time.

CHAPTER 10

Fred Lorenzen

No matter how you look at the map, Elmhurst, Illinois, is one heck of a long way from Charlotte, North Carolina; Daytona Beach, Florida. Martinsville, Virginia—or just about any other place in the traditional stomping grounds of "good ol' boy" southern stock car racing. But somehow that fact didn't have much of an impact on a hometown Elmhurst boy by the name of Fred Lorenzen. The time was the mid-fifties and Lorenzen was then a hot shoe on the mostly midwestern-based United States Auto Club (USAC) stock car circuit. Why not try a bit of NASCAR-style stock car racing, the young Yankee thought; so it was off to the southland with a 1956 Ford that carried the No. 150. Seven races later, Lorenzen found himself headed back north, both broke and discouraged with just one top-twenty finish and a paltry $235 in prize money. Just twenty-two years old (Lorenzen's birthday was December 30, 1934),

Fred Lorenzen signed on with Holman and Moody as one of its first team drivers. By 1962, he was a star on the circuit. His good looks and driving skill caused him to be called NASCAR's "Golden Boy." The Daytona Racing Archives

he still had plenty of time to make a name for himself in NASCAR circles. Once back in the land of Lincoln, he rededicated himself to winning USAC laurels, and he won the USAC stock car championship series back to back in 1958 and 1959 (in a '58 Ford).

With that success as encouragement, Lorenzen once again headed south, this time with a 1960 Ford in tow. At first the results of his second assault on the NASCAR circuit were encouraging. At that year's Daytona 500, he placed third in one of the qualifying races, started in the third row in the 500 itself, and finished a solid eighth place. Even so, shortly after the race, Lorenzen's fortunes once again took a turn for the worse, and by the October running of the Atlanta 500, Lorenzen was just about flat broke. Fact of the matter is, he had already loaded up his independently sponsored Ford (following a tenth place finish in the race) and was ready to head home to Elmhurst. Just as Lorenzen was ready to pull out of the Atlanta track's garage area, a man named Moody approached him. That fellow just happened to be one half of the Holman and Moody racing factory, Ford's official racing arm on the NASCAR circuit. Lorenzen's driving had caught Moody's eye. Better than that, Moody was looking for a new team driver for the 1961 NASCAR season, and was inclined to offer the job to Lorenzen. The offer was made official on Christmas Eve 1960, and at the close of that long distance phone call, Lorenzen's life and the NASCAR history books were changed forever.

The H&M crew did not have a car ready for Lorenzen in time for Daytona Speed Weeks 1961, so he accepted a ride in that race from a fellow with the unlikely name of Tubby Gonzalez. Though Gonzalez' Ford was far from the class of the field, Lorenzen translated a forty-fifth place starting berth into an amazing fourth-place finish. His first turn behind the wheel of a factory-backed H&M Ford came the next month at the Atlanta 500, and with it came the white racing livery and blue No. 28 demarcation that Lorenzen soon made world famous.

Fast Freddie's first official NASCAR win came at the rain-shortened Virginia 500 in Martinsville, Virginia, on April 9. Though the field had only completed a bit more than 25 percent of the laps needed to make up the full event, a hard rain and an unusual official's call resulted in Lorenzen's being assigned the win. Any doubts about that outcome were erased a month later at Darlington, where Lorenzen completed every grueling mile of the 1961 Rebel 300 on his way to edging out Curtis Turner for the win. Turner, in the twilight of his career and badly in need of the winner's share of the purse to help finance his construction effort of the Charlotte Motor Speedway, was said to have been so angered by Lorenzen's win that he rammed into him on the back stretch of the cool-down lap.

Even though Lorenzen seemed to have little trouble defeating veteran southern-bred NASCAR stars like Turner, he often felt he was at a disadvantage to them. According to Lorenzen, southern drivers in those days learned how to drive at ten to twelve years old (indeed, Turner himself often claimed to have made his first delivery of moonshine at the tender age of nine!). On the other hand, Lorenzen basically had to teach himself how to drive competitively, and not until he started racing a hopped-up '52 Olds out of the Elmhurst service station where he worked. When he signed on with H&M in 1961, Ralph Moody became his mentor (and what better teacher could there have been?). Lorenzen proved to be a quick study and soon was besting the "good ol' boys" at their own game. That included stretching the NASCAR rules book a bit now and then, as was the case in the 1962 Atlanta 500. The importance of aerodynamics was lost on many Motown stylists in the early sixties, and in 1962 the Ford styling division had definitely missed the boat. Galaxies that year featured a squared-off formal roof that was about as aerodynamic as a brick. Ford race teams very quickly discovered that "convertible" rooflined cars like Fireball Roberts' No. 22 Catalina were measurably faster on superspeedways.

Enter the creative genius of the Holman and Moody crew and the active cooperation of the folks back in Ford's corporate "glasshouse" headquarters. The result of their conspiracy was the "Starlift" re-

movable roof option that was supposedly an over-the-counter option for 1962 Galaxie convertibles. As you might have guessed, the new replacement roof was as swoopy as a roller coaster ride and it did wonders for a NASCAR Galaxie's top speed. Of course, the fact that a stock street convertible's windows couldn't possibly go all the way up with the new hard top roof in place *did* make the option more than a little suspect. Even so, the sanctioning body allowed Lorenzen's white-and-blue Galaxie to use a "Starlift" roof for the 1962 Atlanta 500, and, of course, he won. Immediately after the race, the same NASCAR officials who had approved the roof outlawed it, and it was never used again. In 1963, Ford stylists permanently cured the problem with a "convertible" style roofline of their own.

In 1965, Fast Freddie won the Daytona 500 in a Holman and Moody '65 Galaxie. Craft Photo

NASCAR cars circa 1965 were a handful and weighed 4,000lbs. We wonder how many modern drivers would be able to muscle one of those beasts around without power steering? Craft Photo

And what a year 1963 was for Fast Freddie and the Holman and Moody team. Paired that year with Fireball Roberts (who joined H&M part way into the season), Lorenzen made good use of both his new Galaxie's slippery silhouette and its new fire-breathing 427ci big-block engine. Lorenzen qualified second for the Daytona 500 and then took second place in a 1-2-3-4-5 place Ford sweep of NASCAR's Super Bowl. Finishing 40 seconds ahead of Lorenzen was Tiny Lund, who won the 500 that year in storybook fashion as a last-minute replacement for Marvin Panch.

Lorenzen's first win of the season came back at Atlanta, where this time he dominated the competition without the aid of a removable roof. Wins in the World 600 at Charlotte, the Volunteer 500 at Bristol, and four other venues—plus a string of top-five finishes—put Lorenzen third in the championship points race and, for the first time in NASCAR history,

paid more than $100,000 in prize money ($122,587.28 to be exact).

Unfortunately, 1964 turned out to be one of tragedy and personal injury for the "Golden Boy" of stock car racing. When the season opened, Lorenzen and the other Ford drivers on the circuit were confronted with a fleet of Mopar rivals that were all powered by a race only 426ci Hemi-headed engine that NASCAR officials had ruled stock even though it would be two full years before a car would ever roll off a UAW assembly line under Hemi power. Richard Petty and his Plymouth and Dodge counterparts pretty much cleaned house that year at Daytona and just about every other superspeedway. Even so, Lorenzen salvaged wins for Ford at Atlanta (where he won his third straight Atlanta 500), North Wilkesboro, Martinsville, and Darlington (where he clinched his second Rebel 300). Then came the ill-fated World 600 that ultimately claimed teammate Fire-

Lorenzen kept fast company in 1965. Here Junior Johnson leads Fast Freddie, Darel Dieringer and Marvin Panch through turn four at Daytona. The Daytona Racing Archives

When Ford opted to sit out the '66 season, Lorenzen signed on with Junior Johnson to drive a creatively configured Galaxie that people called the "Yellow Banana." Though built with a chopped roof, radically raked front clip, and strangely soaring rear deck to enhance aerodynamics, NASCAR still let the car run—one race. Craft Collection

When Ford returned to the circuit late in '66, Fast Freddie was mounted in downsized Fairlanes like this one. Though stubby in appearance, their 427 engines still made them fast. Craft Photo

ball Roberts' life. During their short time together on the Holman and Moody team, Lorenzen had grown very close to Roberts and, according to Lorenzen, Fireball had been his childhood hero even before he turned his first competitive lap. "Fireball was sort of my idol," Lorenzen recently recalled. "When he got killed, it sort of took the racing spirit out of me, sort of like when you finally find out about Santa Claus."

Though Roberts was horribly burned on Memorial Day, he lingered in a Charlotte hospital until just two days before the running of the Firecracker 250. Lorenzen heard the news of Roberts' passing the morning after he had talked to him in the hospital. It had a strong effect on him. According to Lorenzen, "His death changed my driving. I wasn't the same person. . . . I didn't look at racing like I did before his death." Lorenzen's disenchantment with the racing world was, if anything, heightened by a serious

wreck he had while qualifying for the Firecracker just a few days later. As with Roberts' wreck, Lorenzen had the misfortune of being in the way when a shunt was set off by another group of drivers (in this case, Paul Goldsmith, A.J. Foyt, Darel Dieringer, and Johnny Rutherford). Lorenzen got the worst of the affair. The entire left side of his '64 Galaxie was ripped away in the melee and Lorenzen himself suffered a cut artery and a hand injury that required surgery. While laid up in the hospital, Lorenzen's first response was to threaten to retire from competition unless speeds on the track were reduced (Daytona velocities in 1964 were in the 154mph range). Lorenzen ultimately relented, but was forever changed by the experience of Fireball's death coupled with his own near-fatal injuries. He finished out the 1964 season with eight wins and more than $73,000 in winnings, and the hope that things would get better in 1965.

For a while it indeed looked as if Lorenzen's career would get back on track. Speed Weeks 1965 was a successful seven days for Fast Freddie as he finished second in his 100mi qualifier and was running first in the race itself when the February Daytona skies opened up and drenched the track. Three hours after NASCAR officials red-flagged the race, Lorenzen was officially awarded the victory, his first Daytona 500 win.

Nineteen hundred and sixty-five was the year of the Mopar boycott (in response to NASCAR's decision to de-legalize the 426 Hemi engines that had been deemed "stock" just one season before), so Ford drivers such as Lorenzen had little trouble scoring wins. Lorenzen scored four of the forty-eight victories racked up by Blue Oval pilots that season and he pocketed more than $80,000 in winnings (second only to the $93,624 that Ned Jarrett earned as GN champion). This was Lorenzen's last really successful year in NASCAR racing. The next year, 1966, saw Ford drivers sitting on the sideline when the sanctioning body refused to legalize the Ford single overhead camshaft 427 engines, and Lorenzen was only able to start eleven races and win two. Notable in those starts was the one he made for Junior Johnson's independent Ford team at Atlanta in the Dixie 400. In a desperate attempt to keep Ford fans in the grandstands during the Fomoco boycott, NASCAR officials took to loosely interpreting the official rules book where independent-minded Ford owners like Johnson were involved. Junior Johnson cooked up a curvaceous, far-from-stock version of the basic Galaxie race car that people took to calling the "Yellow Banana" due to its severely chopped roofline, strangely tilting deck lid, and radically plunging hoodline. Just as in Lorenzen's "Starlift" days, Johnson was bending the rules book out of shape in search of better aerodynamics. It might have worked too, had third-place qualifier Lorenzen not had a close encounter with the wall on lap 139. After the race, Johnson was told to park his Banana—permanently.

Ford teams officially returned to the circuit late in the season and from then on campaigned downsized intermediate Fairlanes. Lorenzen received one of the new smaller cars, too, and drove it for Holman and Moody for the first part of the 1967 season. He began that year with a win in his Daytona 500 qualifier and a solid second place finish in the race itself (behind Mario Andretti in another Holman and Moody team Fairlane). But 1967 was destined to be King Richard Petty's year of ascension to the NASCAR throne, so Lorenzen and other Ford drivers had a hard time of things. And in April 1967, Lorenzen stunned the racing world by announcing his retirement just after missing the Martinsville race due to ulcers. At the time Lorenzen said, "I want to go out while I'm on top. I've won everything that you can win and there's no way to go but down."

Fast Freddie drove for Holman and Moody until 1967. Though he attempted "comebacks" several years later, he never recaptured the success of his H&M days. Craft Photo

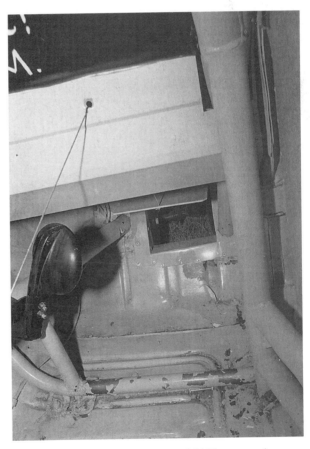

Tires were a major problem in NASCAR's very early years. Even as late as 1967, cars like Lorenzen's Fairlane were equipped with floorboard trap doors and strobe lights, which permitted visual inspection of the right front tire during a race. Craft Photo

Fast Freddie went to work in this cockpit in 1967. Though Spartan, it was a whole lot closer to stock than the ones occupied by Bill Elliott and Mark Martin today. Craft Photo

During one of Lorenzen's comeback attempts in 1970, he drove this red #98 Talladega for Junior Johnson at Darlington. Craft Collection

Lorenzen's '62 Galaxie was handicapped by its nonaero-dynamic rooflines. Ford tried to correct things with a "Starlift" optional roof but was thwarted by NASCAR. In

1963, Galaxies featured sleeker "convertible" rooflines. Petersen Publication Group Archives

His retirement from racing proved to be short-lived, and by 1970 he was considering a comeback. His first attempt came at the World 600, where he finished twenty-fourth after the Hemi in his winged Daytona expired on lap 252. He also campaigned the same No. 28 Dodge in the Firecracker 400 without much better results. Another outing in a winged car at Atlanta, this time for Ray Fox, was also less than successful, as was a run at the Southern 500 in a long-nosed Torino Talladega provided by Junior Johnson. Lorenzen made several more Mopar starts in 1971 (finishing as high as fourth and fifth at tracks like Rockingham and Talladega). He also tried to run

the Southern 500 for the Wood Brothers (in a Mercury), and he bettered the track record in a prerace practice—just before a major wreck thwarted that attempt. Lorenzen finally gave up his comeback hopes in 1972 and returned to Illinois, where he started a lucrative real estate business. Today, Lorenzen admits that his premature retirement in 1967 was a mistake. Of racing, he says, "I miss it a lot. I'm not as happy as I was." Even though it's been more than two decades since Fast Freddie strapped himself into a Grand National car, he still has legions of fans around the circuit, and to them, he will always be the "Golden Bay" of stock car racing.

CHAPTER 11

Banjo Matthews

When Edwin Matthews was just a boy, his eyesight was so bad that he needed thick lenses to correct it. According to some of his perhaps not-so-charitable cronies, the lenses of those glasses were so thick that they resembled twin banjos. And so a lifelong nickname was born. Though corrective surgery would eliminate the need for such thick spectacles later in his life, Matthews never got rid of the nickname and he's been known as Banjo ever since.

Banjo was born on February 14, 1932, in Akron, Ohio, far from the southland and the sport around which he would spend his life. Like many Buckeyes before and since, the Matthews family relocated to sunny south Florida, and by the time Banjo was fifteen, he was racing modifieds at Pompano Beach. He dis-

Banjo Matthews got his start as a driver on the modified circuit in South Florida. The Daytona Racing Archives

played talent as a driver and though just a lad, he won the first race he ever entered. He later became a regular on NASCAR's modified circuit. His best year in that series was 1954 when he won fifty featured events. During his modified career, Banjo won the Daytona race three times, twice on the fabled Beach Course (in 1955 and 1958) and once on Daytona's newly opened superspeedway in 1959.

Later he made the transition to Grand National division racing. One of his earliest appearances on the circuit came at Spartanburg in 1955, when he stepped into the same Frank Christian '55 Chevrolet that Fonty Flock had driven to that manufacturer's first NASCAR win at Columbia three months earlier. It wasn't a full-time "ride," however, and Banjo also ran for other teams that season. Banjo ran at selected races on the circuit until 1962, but he never made it into the winner's circle. He did come close on a number of occasions, and his best finish was a second place at Atlanta in 1962.

Matthews was perhaps a better crew chief and mechanic than he was a driver. For example, while a driver on the modified circuit, he had built and prepared all of his racing machinery. By the end of his driving career in the NASCAR ranks, he had developed quite a reputation as a Grand National mechanic.

It was 1962 when Matthews first tried his luck as a team owner. Fireball Roberts and Smokey Yunick had ended their association just after Fireball's win at the Daytona 500 that year. Following that split, he paired up with Banjo the car owner and campaigned

Matthews drove to modified victories many times. In 1959, his Thunderbird won the first modified race held at Daytona. The Daytona Racing Archives

red, white, and blue Pontiacs at selected races for the balance of the season. Fireball brought Banjo his first win as a team owner in July when he backed up his 500 win with a victory in the Firecracker 200. In addition to backing Roberts that day, Banjo also drove his own No. 02 Poncho in the race. He put his car on the pole and was in contention for the win himself until his engine blew on lap 73 of the 100 that made up the event. Matthews and Roberts remained a team through 1962 and into 1963, when Fireball signed with Holman and Moody in May.

Banjo signed on with Ford's Total Performance Team the next year and prepared cars for A.J. Foyt's limited appearances on the NASCAR circuit. A.J.'s first appearance came at Riverside. One month later at

the Daytona 500 he qualified Matthews' car eighth and lead the race—the only Ford driver to do so during Richard Petty's romp that year—before exiting with engine trouble on lap 127. Junior Johnson took Foyt's seat in Banjo's car when he joined forces with Ford at Martinsville. Junior finished third that day in the Virginia 500 and recorded Banjo's second win as a team owner (and Johnson's thirty-sixth) at the Myers Brother Memorial at Winston-Salem in August. Junior placed his No. 27 Matthews team Galaxie in the winner's circle at Roanoke one day later for his final win of the season.

Johnson left Matthews to field his own cars in 1965 and Banjo picked up driver Bobby Johns. After returning a third place in the Daytona 500 that year,

Eventually, Matthews gave up driving his own cars to work on others. Here he is wrenching on Junior Johnson's '64 Galaxie. *The Daytona Racing Archives*

Johns left and an aggressive young driver named Cale Yarborough took his place. It was Cale's first "big time" ride. He gained fame of an unwanted sort in the Southern 500 when a shunt involving Sam McQuagg's car caused Cale's orange No. 27 to be catapulted over the crash barrier at Darlington and hurled out of the track. Fortunately, Yarborough was only shaken up by his wild ride. A.J. Foyt also made an appearance in a Banjo Matthews Ford that year and won the Firecracker 400 at Daytona.

When Ford teams were instructed to sit out the 1966 season due to a disagreement with Bill France about the legality of the 427 SOHC motor, Banjo's cars were idle until the walkout ended late in the season. He provided the mechanical backing for Ned Jarrett's final NASCAR race at Martinsville after the Ford teams came back. Jarrett, the 1965 GN champ, announced his retirement after returning a third-place finish in the Bondy Long Galaxie. A.J. Foyt drove one of Banjo's Fords at Daytona in 1967, and also drove the Fairlane at Atlanta and in the Firecracker 400, but it was an off-year for the duo and there were no top-ten finishes.

That changed in 1968 when young Donnie Allison, the GN Rookie of the Year for 1967, joined Matthews' team. Allison ran an impressive third in an

Later in his career, Matthews became a team owner. Donnie Allison drove Fords for Banjo during the factory Aero-Wars. Those Talladegas were prepared in Banjo's Asheville, North Carolina, shop. *Craft Collection*

orange fastbacked Torino at Atlanta, third again at Martinsville, and second in the World 600 at Charlotte before finding the key to victory lane at Rockingham. Things were even better for Allison and Matthews in 1969. Team cars grew long noses that year to become Torino Talladegas. Allison quickly put his car's aerodynamic advantage over its Mopar counterparts to good advantage at Daytona, where he led seventy-two of the annual classic's 200 laps on his way to a third-place finish. Allison also was impressive in the 1969 World 600, where he started third place and went on to win when he finished just ahead of his brother Bobby's also-ran Dodge.

Allison stayed with Banjo through the 1970 season and part way into the 1971 tour. Allison won three more times in Matthews' orange Talladega at Bristol, Charlotte (in the World 600 after being relieved by LeeRoy Yarbrough), and Daytona in the Firecracker. Unfortunately for Matthews' efforts as a

Today, Banjo runs Banjo's Performance Center and is responsible for building many of the cars on any starting grid. Banjo's mechanical advice is still highly sought after—even by mechanical wizards like Jack Roush. Craft Photo

Allison's cars were powered by massive 7-liter Boss 429s in '69, '70, and '71. Here, Banjo is running a Boss 429 on an engine stand. Craft Collection

team owner, Ford got out of racing in 1971. Following that corporate departure, Banjo began to focus his efforts on his own race car fabrication company in Arden, North Carolina. It quickly grew to become one of the premier fabrication shops in stock car racing and scores of winning cars of all makes have been built there. Banjo's Performance Center is still in operation today and continues to be one of the top race car shops in the country.

Chapter 12

Ralph Moody

*C*ircle Track magazine has called Ralph Moody "every crew chief's godfather," and that's one bit of journalistic hyperbole that is on the mark. But that wasn't Moody's goal when he first got into racing as a Taunton, Massachusetts, teenager.

He just liked to go fast. Perhaps there was a bit of youthful rebellion there, too, since his dad, Ralph, Sr., looked with great disdain upon racing. In fact, the elder Moody's opposition to his son's tinkering with high-performance motorcycles and cars eventually led Ralph, Jr., to move to his grandparent's house at age fourteen. While living with them in Littleton, Massachusetts, Moody and a friend took in a midget race at the Boston Garden. It proved to be a turning point in Moody's life, and after the race he and his friend bought a wreck and returned it to the track. Though Moody would later gain fame as a mechanic, his job in that racing partnership was that of driver. As things turned out, he was a pretty darned good one.

During the thirties, Moody gained fame for his midget driving on the dirt tracks of New England. In time, he even earned the approval of his father, though at first Moody was forced to race under as-

sumed names for fear that his dad would find out. As mentioned, Moody was more than a passable driver and he won the New England Midget Championship in his fourth year on the circuit. Strictly stock "jalopies" and modifieds came next, and Moody once again ran at the front of the pack. He won eleven straight features at Norwood, Massachusetts, with his '40 Ford coupe, for example, and was actually barred from the track for being too successful.

Though Moody was quite adept at collecting racing purses, he also set up a car and engine repair service where he began to perfect his native mechanical genius. "I found out that you can have all the motor you want," Moody said," but if you can't point the car in the right direction, the way you want it to go, you're not going to be a winner." In time Moody became one of the most respected "chassis" men in racing. Ultimately the handling and braking modifications he introduced would revolutionize the sport of stock car racing. Moody was one of the first (if not *the* first) to employ weight jacks to fine tune a race car's handling. Prior to their introduction, sophisticated mechanics of the day would often get all of their friends to stand on one side or

Ralph Moody got his start as a driver, but by 1957 he'd hooked up with John Holman to found Holman and Moody (H&M). Here, he chats it up with Dodge team owner Cotton Owens (right). The Daytona Racing Archives

One of Ralph Moody's favorite stock cars was the #12 Cyclone Bobby Allison drove for Holman and Moody in 1971. Craft Collection

other of the car while the suspension was chained in place. Moody is also directly responsible for the double-centered racing hubs and massive Lincoln-derived drum brakes that were used on almost every Grand National stock car from the mid-fifties to the advent of the disc brakes in the early seventies. Ditto for the Galaxie-based front chassis snout that Moody perfected in 1965. In fact, the handful of rear steer cars still on the circuit use Moody's basic front chassis design and geometry. Moody has also been credited with helping to design the first successful racing shock absorber capable of withstanding stock car abuse.

But all of those mechanical achievements came after Moody the driver made a mark for himself on the NASCAR circuit. After Army Air Corps service in World War II, Moody headed south to Ft. Lauderdale, Florida, where he opened a speed shop. He stayed active in racing and soon was a star driver at the Opa Locka speedway (where incidentally, a young spectator named Bobby Allison would later also become quite well known). At one point Moody won eighteen straight races there.

Moody's first NASCAR ride came in 1965 when he went to Daytona to check on the possibility of securing a factory Pontiac ride. While there, he visited Fireball Roberts, who was driving for Pete DePaolo's Ford factory team. As luck would have it, Speedy Thompson had just left the team and Moody was asked to fill his seat for the beach race a few days later. It was Moody's big break and the start of an association with Ford that would last until 1972. Though Moody only qualified his No. 12 Ford in the twenty-second position, by midrace he was running with the leaders. Even a flip on the sandy beach portion of the 4.1mi-long track wasn't enough to keep him from finishing third that day. After the race, Moody's brief bit of "air time" was featured in *Life* magazine in a dramatic photo. Moody's performance also got the attention of the folks in Dearborn, and he was offered a factory ride for the balance of the season. Moody moved to Charlotte and began to make regular appearances on the 1956 race circuit.

NASCAR racing was a rough-and-tumble affair in those days and early stars like Curtis Turner and Joe Weatherly were not above intentionally putting a

John Holman was one half of the fabled Holman and Moody concern. Here he poses with a Holman and Moody '63 Ford NASCAR chassis. Petersen Publication Group Archives

speeding truck's path. When the 1957 season got under way, the supercharged Fairlanes that Moody, Joe Weatherly, Fireball Roberts, and others campaigned were still referred to as DePaolo team cars, but by July that designation had been changed to Holman and Moody. Formed just as Ford exec Robert McNamara was being snookered into getting out of factory-backed racing by the GM-concocted AMA (Automobile Manufacturers of America) ban on factory motorsports, Holman and Moody received most of the Ford race cars and equipment when the corporation pulled out of the series. Before that departure, Ford drivers had won nineteen of the first twenty-eight 1957 GN races. Moody had played a driving role in six races that season, winning one and posting top-five finishes in four others. Though Moody probably didn't know it at the time, his first win over Buck Baker at Wilson, North Carolina, was to be the fifth and final win of his Grand National driving career. Overseeing the mechanical operations at Holman and Moody would soon take him from be-

competitor out of an event while "guarding their turf." At times, Moody as a Yankee (who still retains traces of his Massachusetts accent today) often received special attention from Little Joe and "Pops" Turner. Moody recalls that at one race "Turner tried to knock me off of the track. I recovered and got him in the infield. I called his bluff. After the race, I went up to him and jerked him off of a pickup truck by the neck. We were good friends after that. Not only was I an outsider, I was competition." And indeed he was. By the close of his first Grand National season, Moody had scored victories at four races (his first coming in a 250-miler at Memphis that was marred by two fatalities) and had finished in the top five at nine others. He was eighth in points that year.

Nineteen hundred and fifty-six was also the first year that Moody paired up with John Holman. Pete DePaolo initially had control of Ford's factory-backed racing effort in 1956, but by the end of the year Holman had been brought in to make the team function more efficiently. Holman was a former truck driver who possessed a large amount of business savvy. He had driven the supply truck for Lincoln-Mercury's successful Carrera Panamericana road racing effort, earning the nickname "Honker" for his heavy use of a diesel horn to clear donkeys and natives from his

Moody's genius also was largely responsible for the Torino Talladegas that won the factory-backed Aero-Wars in 1969 and 1970. Here, H&M team driver David Pearson (center) poses with Fomoco drivers Richard Petty, Cale Yarborough, Donnie Allison, and LeeRoy Yarbrough in 1969. Craft Collection

hind the wheel of a race car for good. But it was probably a fair trade-off, for over the next fifteen NASCAR seasons Moody's mechanical genius played a primary role in the 1992 Grand National wins and two national championships won by Holman and Moody drivers, and scores more turned in by non-team drivers in H&M built cars. (At one time, H&M was responsible for building most, if not all, Ford and Mercury race cars for Grand National, ARCA, and USAC competition.) His expertise also helped Ford corporate racers win dozens of NHRA drag races, sports car races, and Le Mans, since many of Ford's fastest non-NASCAR cars were also developed and built at H&M's sprawling Charlotte airport complex.

In 1958, Moody and H&M began building customer race cars (a first in an era when most racers built their cars in a backyard garage) as well as continuing to build cars for their own team drivers. Curtis Turner recorded the first H&M GN win at Fayetteville in March 1958. Unit body Thunderbirds were some of the first H&M customer cars built, and Hol-

man used his relationship with Ford to secure "bodies in white" straight off the assembly line to serve as the basis for their construction. This was also a precursor of the days when racers would no longer buy their race cars off the showroom floor but instead would purpose-build them from scratch.

In addition to his mechanical acuity, Moody also had a pretty fair eye for driving talent. Many of the drivers he picked to campaign H&M team cars became some of the greatest in Grand National history. In 1960, he was impressed with the way an independent young driver from Elmhurst, Illinois, handled his home-built Ford, and offered him a job at H&M. That fellow's name was Fred Lorenzen, and he quickly became the Golden Boy of Grand National racing in his Holman and Moody Galaxies.

In 1962, when (having fortuitously lost McNamara to the Kennedy administration—where he saw the light at the end of the Vietnam tunnel) Ford decided to return to full-time, factory-backed motorsports competition, Holman and Moody became the

Ralph Moody signed Fred Lorenzen as an H&M team driver. In 1965, Fast Freddie drove a competition-proven Galaxie to victory at the Daytona 500. Craft Photo

Dick Hutcherson was first a team H&M driver, then David Pearson's crew chief and finally shop foreman at Holman and Moody. Much of what he learned there was translated into the race cars his Hutcherson-Pagan shop began building when H&M closed down in 1972. The Daytona Racing Archives

Holman and Moody closed its doors in 1972. This is the last H&M car ever built. It was campaigned by Bobby Unser at Riverside. Craft Photo

official factory racing arm in the South. Those were truly glory days for Moody and H&M. Their shop literally built fleets of Ford and Mercury race cars (up to eighty a year) and high-performance engines by the truckload. In time, almost every car on the circuit, regardless of manufacture, sported at least a few H&M components. Mechanical innovations introduced by Moody even influenced the official NASCAR rules book when they proved to be safer (and usually faster) than earlier equipment.

During the sixties and seventies, H&M backed Lorenzen, Fireball Roberts, David Pearson, Nelson Stacey, Bobby Allison, Dick Hutcherson, and Dan Gurney, and they each parked H&M "Competition Proven" cars in the winner's circle at NASCAR events. Pearson won Holman and Moody's two GN championships in 1968 and 1969.

In late 1968, when the factory wars were reaching their peak, Moody helped find a Ford counter to the new aerodynamically improved Dodges that were to be unveiled in 1969. Working in the backroom at H&M on his own and in concert with Ford engineers, Moody grafted on a new droopy nose to the standard 1968 Torino unit body and created the Talladega. The car went on to beat the new Dodge aero cars—even after they sprouted wings and beaks to become Dodge Daytonas—and sweep the 1969 season. That was also the year that Moody and H&M persuaded NASCAR to permit the use of fabricated (rather than factory) frame members—which, of course, is standard operating procedure in Winston Cup today. Unfortunately, that was essentially Ford's last year of triumph on the NASCAR circuit. When new Ford chief Lee Iacocca decided to cut Ford's racing budget by 75 percent across the board for 1970 and end it altogether in 1971, Ford's and Holman and Moody's glory days were surely over. Though Bobby Allison won a string of superspeedway races with a 1969 Cyclone (that Moody still recalls as his favorite race car) during the 1971 season, by 1972 H&M was essentially out of the business. Though Moody and Holman had forged an empire that extended to racing fabrication shops in California, a marine racing shop in Florida, and catalog sales of high-performance parts exceeding those of any other high-performance builder (including a contract with Sears to distribute H&M parts through that retailer's own catalog), on a personal level they were not great friends. When the factory sponsorship glue (read: money) that had kept them together dried up, the two went their separate ways and H&M closed its doors for good.

Ralph Moody is retired and lives not far from the Charlotte airport H&M complex. Craft Photo

Today Moody lives in Charlotte and enjoys a well-deserved retirement. His influence on the sport of stock car racing cannot be understated since the mechanical changes he helped introduce literally changed the face of racing forever.

Bud Moore

The sign on the red brick building just down the road from sleepy little Converse College in Spartanburg reads: "Bud Moore Engineering." Just inside the door are walls covered with the photos and racing memorabilia of Walter "Bud" Moore's four-decade-long racing career. But conspicuously absent in that colorful display is a framed college degree. Moore, a tall and sometimes reticent man, smiles when asked from which college he got his engineering degree.

"I got my education right here," he replies as he points to the floor of his race team's shop. Born in 1925 and raised during the hard scrabble years of the Depression, Moore never had the chance to acquire much formal education. There may have been times when that caused Moore, a native of Spartanburg, South Carolina, to feel a little self-conscious, but those days are long since gone. After all, why feel embarrassed by the lack of a college degree when major automakers send their college-trained engineers to Moore's shop to seek his advice?

Like many in his generation, Moore responded to Uncle Sam's call during World War II and at nineteen was one of the first American soldiers to storm Utah Beach on D-Day. After making it ashore that day, Moore followed in the wake of old "Blood and Guts" General Patton across the continent. In six months of fighting, Moore saw action in five major battles, received two Purple Hearts, two Bronze Stars, and was promoted to the rank of sergeant. After the war, Moore returned to South Carolina and found work in the automotive trade. In time, he was working on cars for the local modified race car drivers. Though not a driver himself, Moore had an uncanny ability to make a race car go fast.

His talents with a wrench came to the attention of teams on the new-at-the-time NASCAR Grand National tour, and by 1956, Moore was the chief mechanic for Buck Baker's factory-backed Chevrolet race team. Moore's mechanical support made it possible for Baker's fuel-injected No. 87 Chevy to win ten Grand National events and finish in the top ten at twenty-eight others. It was a championship-winning performance, and for the second straight year Baker was the best driver in NASCAR's premier division. It was not the last time that Moore would provide the mechanical backing for a Grand National championship.

In the fifties, Moore also worked as a crew chief on the cars of Speedy Thompson and Jack Smith, and in 1961 Moore started his own team. Pontiac was the hot car on the circuit that year and the back

Moore is still providing cars for top NASCAR drivers today. Morgan Shepherd drove a Motorcraft Ford for Moore, for example. Craft Collection

door to its racing division was wide open to NASCAR team owners like Moore. Joe Weatherly was the driver that season of Moore's No. 8 Pontiacs, and the two were successful immediately. The new team's first race was the second Daytona qualifier that year. Little Joe qualified the No. 8 car first for the 100mi affair and won the race that was marred by Lee Petty and Johnny Beauchamp's now-famous fourth turn wreck (which saw both cars hurtle outside of the speedway). In the 500 itself, Weatherly started on the outside of the front row and ran well en route to a second-place finish.

Weatherly made Moore a two-time race-winning team owner at Charlotte when he beat Junior Johnson's Pontiac in one of the qualifying races that used to be run for the World 600. Weatherly won seven more times for the team that year, including triumphs at Martinsville, Bristol, and Charlotte. He also finished in the top ten at nine more races, and finished fourth in the championship standings. All in all, it was a phenomenal first year for Moore's team.

Moore, Weatherly, and Pontiac remained a team for 1962 and had another extremely good year. Weatherly backed up his nine 1961 wins with nine more in Moore's 421 Super Duty-powered Catalina. The extra points racked up in thirty-six other top-ten finishes made the difference in the points race, and Weatherly finished more than 2,000 points ahead of Richard Petty to take the title.

The team stayed together for 1963 and by April, Weatherly had parked Moore's car in victory lane again (at Richmond). Unfortunately, 1963 was the year that General Motors finally honored the AMA ban on factory racing that it had engineered in 1957 (as a way to put Ford on the sidelines). When Pontiac cut back its racing budget, Moore was no longer able to run the full series, so Weatherly—in hot pursuit of his second GN championship—was forced to bum rides from other car owners at the races Moore didn't enter. Little Joe won for Moore at Darlington in the Rebel 300 and Hillsboro, and those victories, combined with the points he had hustled (for Moore

Bud Moore came home from WWII and got involved in the used car business. By the mid-fifties he'd been the chief mechanic on many top flight Grand National cars.

His Spartanburg shop carries on that winning tradition today. Craft Collection

In 1966, Moore built an innovative downsized Comet that Darel Dieringer drove to victory in the Southern 500. The Daytona Racing Archives

The 427 engines Moore built for Joe Weatherly's Mercury Marauders (background) helped Little Joe win the '63 Winston Cup championship. Craft Photo

Little Joe Weatherly was driving a Bud Moore engineering Mercury like this one when he lost his life in 1964. Craft Collection

Moore was one of the first to build a "half-chassis" car in 1966. That innovative move away from stock led directly to the fully fabricated race cars used in NASCAR today. Craft Collection

and a number of other car owners), helped him win the 1963 championship race. When Little Joe drove his No. 8 Mercury (Moore had picked up a Fomoco sponsorship late in the season to begin the Ford affiliation he still maintains), he was Grand National champ for a second straight year.

Tragically, he was only able to savor that triumph for two short months. When the series returned to Riverside in January 1964, Weatherly lost his life when his red and black No. 8 Marauder left the track on turn six and made heavy contact with the wall. Weatherly never wore a shoulder harness out of fear it would impede his escape from a burning wreck. That decision cost him his life that day when his head flew outside the car and hit the wall during the wreck. Billy Wade filled Weatherly's seat that year and won for Moore: the Fireball Roberts 200 (honor-

ing Fireball, who had been fatally burned in a fiery World 600 wreck) at Old Bridge, New Jersey; the road race at Bridgehampton (that's right, NASCAR did hold road races with lumbering 4,000-plus-pound 1960s stock cars!); the road race at Watkins Glen; and a short track race.

Unfortunately, there was still more tragedy for the team when Moore and Wade went to Daytona in January 1965 for a tire test session. During a ten-lap run, Wade's No. 1 Mercury slammed into the outside wall in turn one, careened down to the apron and then back up into the wall again. When rescue teams reached the promising young driver—the rookie of the year in 1963—he was already dead.

Moore signed Daryl Dieringer to drive for the team following Wade's death and changed the car's number a third time to No. 16. During Speed Weeks

Moore was also instrumental in the move from big-block engines to small-block power. The Fords he built in the mid-seventies were fast even with "baby" motors. Craft Photo

In 1967, Moore left NASCAR to campaign Mercury Cougars on the Trans-Am circuit. In 1970, Moore-prepared Boss Mustangs won the SCCA championship. Craft Collection

1965, Dieringer won a qualifying race for the 500 and was running second behind Fred Lorenzen in the race itself when rain brought the field to a halt. Lorenzen was awarded the rain-shortened race later in the day. Dieringer ultimately scored fourteen top-ten finishes for Moore in 1965 and finished the season third in championship points.

The year of the Ford NASCAR boycott was 1966, and Moore dutifully sat out the first part of the season in response to corporation orders. By midseason, though, Moore was back at the track, campaigning a diminutive little Mercury Comet. When the season began Moore and the other Fomoco teams had planned to campaign the same block-long, "full-sized" race cars they had run in the past. During the boycott, Moore took the pioneering step of building one of NASCAR's first half-chassis cars—that is to say a unit body intermediate that had been spliced together with the front frame member of a full-sized car. Under normal circumstances, NASCAR might have been disinclined to let such a car run. But in light of the Fomoco boycott and the sanctioning body's desperation to attract at least a few Fords to the series, Moore's little Comet was allowed to run. And run it did. The little red, white, and black bullet's first outing came at the Firecracker 400 and Dieringer narrowly missed a win when he ran out of gas on the last lap and coasted to second. He did make it all the way to victory lane with the car at Weaverville, and dominated the field at Darlington on his way to victory in the Southern 500. With this proof of the half-chassis Ford's competitive ability, the rest of Ford's racers also fielded intermediates when they returned to the series later in the year.

Ford called Moore away from the Grand National series in 1967 and put him in charge of campaigning the Lincoln-Mercury Cougar team on the new Trans-Am circuit. His fleet of black-and-gold Cougars was driven by Dan Gurney, Rufus Parnelli Jones, and Ed Leslie. They were ultimately so successful that Ford drivers nearly didn't win the SCCA championship that year. Perhaps as a direct result, there was no Cougar Trans-Am team the following year. Instead, Moore took his little Cougars and entered them at NASCAR Grand American races with Tiny Lund driving. The "Baby Grand" series was Bill France's answer to the SCCA T/A series and ran in conjunction with Grand National races at selected tracks on the circuit. Lund was the Grand American champion that year and he also campaigned a red, white, and black No. 16 Mercury Cyclone for Moore at selected Grand National events.

In 1969, Ford called Moore back to the Trans-Am circuit, this time to campaign Fomoco's all-new Boss 302 Trans-Am cars. Corporate teams had lost the SCCA title for the first time in 1968 (to a couple of Chevrolet racers named Penske and Donohue), and the folks in Dearborn's "Glass House" wanted it back. Moore campaigned two red, black, and white

Mustangs that season for Parnelli and George Follmer. They had to contend with not only the GM competition but also with the other Boss team fielded by Carroll Shelby. Things went well initially for both Ford teams, and for a time it seemed as if the title would be decided between Moore's and Shelby's drivers. Until, that is, a freak wreck at St. Jovite, Canada, eliminated and totally destroyed just about every Boss Mustang on both teams. Penske and Donohue won for a second season as a result.

In 1970 Ford folded its tent and began to leave all forms of factory-backed motorsports. Even so, Moore's Trans-Am team survived the corporation's withering budget cuts; Shelby's team didn't. Switching to school bus-yellow 1970 Boss 302s sporting

In 1968, Moore teamed with driver Tiny Lund. Lund won NASCAR's "Grand American" pony car championship and also drove a Cyclone at selected Grand National events. Craft Collection

Moore still supervises the mechanical work behind his Ford Winston Cup cars. Craft Photo

No. 15 and No. 16 that year, Jones and Follmer finally won back the Trans-Am title Ford had "owned" (save for 1968 and 1969) since that road course series was initiated. Though Ford pulled the financial plug altogether in 1971, Moore kept his team cars and soldiered on for another season as an independent.

When he returned to the NASCAR circuit in 1972, it was a far different place from the one he had left. Restrictor plates (which first reared their ugly heads during the 1970 season) were in widespread use, and the big-block engines they were assigned to by the sanctioning body were sorely burdened. But Moore noticed that small-block motors, should anyone attempt to campaign them, wouldn't be hurt so much (or at all) by NASCAR's accursed restrictor plates. Coming off of three years of firsthand experience with Ford's cant-valved small-block engines (from which he had been able to coax a healthy 650hp in 5-liter form!), Moore thought he was just

Geoff Bodine also drove Thunderbirds for Bud Moore's team. Craft Photo

Moore's Thunderbirds picked up Ford Quality Care racing livery in 1993. Craft Collection

the man to introduce small-block engines to the modern era of NASCAR racing. He was right.

The white No. 15, 351 Cleveland-powered Torinos he built for Donnie Allison, Bobby Isaac, Darrell Waltrip, George Follmer, and Buddy Baker in the mid-seventies didn't exactly set the racing world on its ear, but they did show the way to the future. Today, the big-block engines of old are as dead as the dodo bird in NASCAR racing. An interesting bit of history was made by Bobby Isaac and a Bud Moore small-block Ford in 1973, however. It was at Talladega that year that Isaac, the 1970 GN champ, decided to retire—right in the middle of the race! One can only wonder what Moore said when Isaac pulled into the pits and got out. A fresh-faced kid named Darrell Waltrip took Isaac's place behind the wheel at races later that season.

Moore's small-block-powered Fords won their first race in 1975 when Buddy Baker won the Tal-

ladega 500. If small-block motors could win at Talladega, then they could win anywhere, and soon they were doing just that. Baker recorded two more superspeedway wins for Moore before Bobby Allison took his place in 1978. During Bobby A's tenure as team driver, Moore put fourteen more trophies on his mantle, including one from the Daytona 500. Benny Parson added two more in 1981, and Ricky Rudd earned six in his Moore-built Motorcraft Thunderbirds. Morgan Shepherd and Geoff Bodine are the two most recent drivers to post team wins for Moore. All told, Moore's cars have won forty-two NASCAR races and more than $9 million in earnings.

Moore continues to be one of the top Ford team owners in NASCAR racing today, and his son Greg has joined him in overseeing their North Fairview Avenue operation in Spartanburg.

Cotton Owens

Everett Owens was just a "towheaded" slip of a boy when he began climbing trees outside of the Piedmont, South Carolina, fairgrounds to steal a glimpse of what was going on inside. While other boys his age might have been excited about getting a peek at a traveling circus, or perhaps a livestock display, young Everett (a boy whose hair was so blond that folks called him Cotton) climbed trees at the fairgrounds to watch the car races. His interest in things automotive came naturally since his father was employed as mechanic.

After a brief stint in the war-time Navy, Owens returned to South Carolina and took up his father's trade. One of his first jobs was for a towing and salvage operation that by chance happened to sponsor modified racing standout Gober Sosbee. Before long, Owens was working on Sosbee's car and making plans to go racing himself.

In 1947, he made those plans come to life at a modified race in Hendersonville, North Carolina. He had traveled to the track with Sosbee that day. When Gober came in from a shake-down lap with complaints that his race car wasn't handling right, Owens offered to take it out for a few "diagnostic"

Cotton Owens got his start in racing behind the wheel of a modified car. He later scored Grand National victories. The Daytona Racing Archives

laps. Though it was his first time behind the wheel of a race car on a dirt track, he muscled the car around the track like a veteran. Owens' test laps turned into a ride at the race and he finished second overall.

Owens remained in modifieds for a number of years. He did well, and in 1950 he won fifty-four races. Twenty-four of those victories came back-to-back. His car of choice in those days was a Dodge, and that Mopar preference was to follow him for most of the rest of his racing career. In 1950, Owens had made an outing in the Grand National division at the inaugural Southern 500 at Darlington. He qualified his No. 71 Plymouth an unpromising thirty-eighth but finished in seventh place—a finish that placed him well ahead of such future series stars as Tim Flock, Marshall Teague, Buck Baker, and Curtis Turner. Even so, he remained in the modified ranks and eventually won that series' 1953 and 1954 national championships.

Though Owens ran at selected Grand national events (usually in Hudsons), it wasn't until 1957 that he began to make a mark for himself in the premier NASCAR division. He signed on with Pontiac as a team driver that season and traveled south to Florida

In the sixties, Owens became a team owner. He specialized in cars of the Dodge persuasion. The Daytona Racing Archives

in February to run the 160mi beach race at Daytona. Banjo Matthews sat on the pole that day in another factory Poncho and Cotton qualified third. During the race, Owens quickly took command and led every lap until he had to pit for service. After making a quick (for the day) sixty-one-second stop, Owens rocketed back on the track and into the lead. His primary competition that day was Paul Goldsmith in a Smokey Yunick-prepped '57 Chevrolet. When Goldsmith's engine gave up on lap sixty, Owens had smooth sailing until the checkered flag ended the race. It was both Owens' and Pontiac's first NASCAR Grand National win. Owens turned in six more top-ten finishes in 1957, including a second place in the Southern 500. Owens stayed with Pontiac in 1958 and drove a No. 6 Poncho for Stephens Pontiac of Daytona Beach, Florida. Win number two of his GN career came that season on the dirt track in Rochester, New York. Owens won again in 1959 at Richmond, driving the interestingly named "Thunder Chicken" 1959 Thunderbird. Owens also became the

first driver to top 143mph at Bill France's all new superspeedway in Daytona that year.

Perhaps more important than Owens' record-setting pace and one GN win in 1959 was his decision that same year to set out on his own as a race team owner. At first, Owens drove the cars that he built in his shop, but eventually he began to provide rides for other drivers, too, especially for races on long tracks. In 1961, Owens drove to four more GN victories, including his first as a car owner. Fittingly, that win came at a dirt track in Owens' hometown of Spartanburg. Owens sat on the pole that day in his No. 5 Pontiac and went on to beat Lee Petty to the checkered flag.

At 1962 races where Owens didn't drive, he provided rides for Junior Johnson. Johnson's best finish for Owens was a second in the 1962 Firecracker 250. David Pearson also took up residence in a Cotton Owens-prepped car for the first time in 1962. That would eventually prove to be a fortuitous pairing. Nineteen hundred and sixty-two was the last year for

David Pearson drove for Owens in 1966. His #6 Chargers were tough to beat that year. The Daytona Racing Archives

Owens and Pontiac, and in November he returned to the Mopar cars (in this case Dodges) that he had driven on the modified circuit. Billy Wade also drove for Owens in 1963, but no wins were recorded.

That changed in 1964 when Pearson brought home eight first-place trophies for Dodge and Owens. Jim Paschal, Earl Balmer, and Bobby Isaac also drove Owens-prepped Dodges at some races. Owens himself came out of driving retirement to win the Capital City 300 at Richmond, scoring his ninth and final Grand National win. He said the decision to run that day was more out of love for the fast-disappearing dirt track races on the tour than the desire to win. "I love the dirt tracks," he said after the race. "We're running fewer and fewer dirt tracks on the Grand National circuit these days. That's a shame. I don't care anything about driving on asphalt, I just did it for the fun." He also ran one other race that season.

Owens continued to campaign factory-backed Dodges in 1965, or at least, would have had it not been for the Dodge and Plymouth boycott of the GN series. Big Bill France and the sanctioning body had decided to reverse themselves and disallow the racing Hemi engine for 1965 (after allowing that non-production engine to run in 1964) and Chryco execs decided to sit out the season in protest. Instead of running in circles, Owens and Pearson campaigned a drag race Dodge (called the "Cotton Picker," for obvious reasons).

When the Mopar walkout ended in 1966, Owens and Pearson were a force to be reckoned with. After ironing out their '66 Charger's aerody-

namic deficiencies with a rear deck spoiler (the first allowed in NASCAR), by the end of the season they had won fifteen races (with four coming consecutively) and the 1966 Grand National championship.

Pearson began the 1967 season with Owens in the No. 6 team Dodge but left in April to take the Holman and Moody Ford slot vacated by retiring star Fred Lorenzen. So Owens hired the fiercely independent Bobby Allison. Allison scored Owens' second win of the season (Pearson having won at Bristol) at Birmingham before he returned to his own Chevrolet. Sam McQuagg, Ray Hendrick, Buddy Baker, and Darel Dieringer traded places in Owens' Dodge for the rest of the year without much success.

Indy ace Al Unser drove for Owens at Daytona in 1968 and "tagged out" to Chargin' Charlie Glotzbach. Glotzbach spent the rest of the season in the car and won for Owens and Dodge at the National 500 in Charlotte. It was a rare bright spot for Dodge in a Ford year on the tour. The factory backed "Aero-Wars" broke out in 1969 and Owens campaigned Charger 500s with Glotzbach returning as driver. Chargin' Charlie came in second behind LeeRoy Yarbrough's winning Talladega in the Daytona 500. But 1969 turned out to be yet another Fomoco year in Grand National racing. James Hylton and Buddy Baker drove for Cotton in 1969, too. But the closest any of Owens' drivers got to victory lane

Owens was an expert at making a 426 Hemi perform. The Daytona Racing Archives

After NASCAR permitted the addition of a rear deck spoiler (a first in Grand National racing), Pearson's Cotton Owens-prepared Chargers won the '66 Grand National championship. The Daytona Racing Archives

was the second Baker scored at the Firecracker 400. Not even the new wings and noses his 500s grew at mid-season (to become Daytonas) were enough to help Owens overcome the Ford aero-onslaught. For a time during the last race of the year at Texas, it did seem as though Baker would finally bring home a team victory, but a bit of daydreaming on his part caused Owens' No. 6 Daytona to run into the back of a lapped car while Baker was leading—ending all chance for victory.

Sam Posey (of all people) drove Owens' car in the 1970 season opener at Riverside, but with lackluster results, and Buddy Baker resumed his driver's chores at Daytona. With Ford and Mercury teams suffering under a 75 percent cut in their racing budget, things had to get better for Owens and the other Mopar teams in 1970, and ultimately they did. Baker found victory lane in September at the Southern 500 in Darlington for Owens' first win in several seasons.

The Aero-Wars were over in 1971, thanks to a rules book change, and with Ford out of NASCAR racing altogether, Dodge and Plymouth took the op-

portunity to trim their factory-backed teams. Owens' driver that year was Pete Hamilton, and Hamilton immediately won for the team by putting Owens' No. 6 Plymouth Road Runner in victory lane at one of the two Daytona 500 qualifying races. Unfortunately, engine failure sidelined Hamilton in the 500 itself. Though Hamilton turned in eleven more top-ten finishes, he was not able to find his way back to victory lane that year.

Glotzbach returned in 1972, but by then the flow of factory dollars had slowed to just a fraction of what it had been during the high point of the factory-backed NASCAR wars. Wins were not forthcoming and Dick Brooks wasn't able to improve that situation when he ran for Owens in the 1973 500. After providing the mechanical backing for country music star and sometime racer Marty Robbins during the late seventies, Owens left the track for good. By the middle of the next decade, the championship Dodges that Owens had once fielded were just a memory along pit lane, and Owens retired to his Spartanburg, South Carolina, garage, which he still operates today.

Buddy Baker drove for Owens during the Aero-Wars. Here, Baker and Owens celebrate after winning the 1970 Southern 500. The Daytona Racing Archives

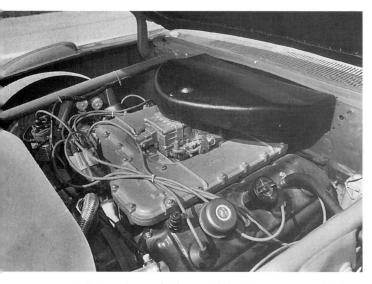

A Cotton Owens-built Hemi like this one powered Baker's Daytona to victory in the Southern 500. Craft Photo

David Pearson

"Little David" and "The Silver Fox" are two nicknames that were used to describe David Pearson during his 105-win Grand National/Winston Cup career, and both were accurate at the time.

During his earliest days of racing, local promoters liked to call Pearson "Little David" because of his ability to show up at a dirt track bull ring and slay the hometown Goliath. That's just how Pearson made his big break into the Grand National ranks at the World 600, where he drove Ray Fox's Catalina as an unknown, last-minute replacement and knocked off all the NASCAR giants of the day to win the event. Years later, after he had amassed many of the NASCAR victories that currently rank him second to only Richard Petty on the all-time win list, the press started calling him the Silver Fox.

It was an appellation that referred both to his graying mane and his canny ability to lie in wait during a race, only to pounce on the win at just the right moment.

Pearson's racing career had a humble start in Spartanburg, South Carolina, with a '40 Ford coupe

Pearson's salt-and-pepper mane, coupled with cagey driving, earned him the nickname "The Silver Fox" during the seventies. Craft Photo

that had a quality that just made people want to pass it. Few of them did, however, and Pearson won just about everyone of the, er, informal back country road races he ran. Pearson's first formal entry at a race came at age seventeen in 1952 when he ran in a hobby race at Woodruff, South Carolina. Today Pearson still laughs about that first outing.

"We didn't know how to prepare the car. We didn't know how to jimmy the suspension. We did it by getting a bunch of fellows to stand on the left side while we tied it down with chains." What Pearson lacked initially in knowledge he more than made up for with courage and native driving skill. Pearson quickly became the terror of the Carolina short tracks and won hundreds of events, including thirty of forty-two events entered during his first year in NASCAR's sportsman division.

By 1959, Pearson had set sights on the NASCAR big leagues, the Grand National series (nee Winston Cup). He made his first GN foray as an independent racer at the 1960 Daytona 500. Pearson spent all of his money and then some getting his '59 Chevy ready to run. He says

David Pearson took advantage of Ford's absence from Grand National racing in 1966 to win the championship in his Cotton Owens-prepared Charger. The Daytona Racing Archives

When Fred Lorenzen retired in 1967, Pearson joined Ford's "Total Performance Team" and Holman and Moody. One year later, he won his second Grand National championship. The Daytona Racing Archives

now, "If I had known then what I know now, I would have never have bought that car. It had run its course." Even so, Pearson turned in a creditable eighteenth-place finish in what was both his first GN outing and first superspeedway appearance. By the end of his career, Pearson had become the all-time superspeedway pole winner, capturing sixty-four such poles; the all-time winner at Darlington and Michigan; the first man to win NASCAR's famed Grand Slam by taking trophies at all of the South's superspeedways (Daytona, Atlanta, Charlotte and Darlington); the conqueror of fifty-one superspeedway victories overall; and the first driver in history to win more than $200,000 in prize money.

Pearson's first big break came while driving for Ray Fox in the 1961 World 600. Despite signing to drive that race less than a week before the green flag fell, Pearson scored one of the biggest upsets in NASCAR history by beating such luminaries as Fireball Roberts, Joe Weatherly, Curtis Turner, and Junior Johnson. Four weeks later he won the Firecracker 400 to become the first driver to win two of the series' major races in one season. Pearson's competitive mount for those races was a No. 3 Pontiac, a brand that he also piloted at different times for car owners Fox, Bud Moore, and Cotton Owens.

In 1962, Pearson hooked up with another Spartanburg mechanic, Cotton Owens, and for the next four years he and Owens campaigned Dodges. A big year for the team was 1966 as Pearson campaigned a fastback-rooflined, Hemi-powered Dodge Charger. Pearson and Owens had been on the NASCAR sidelines during 1965 due to the Chryco boycott of the series (Pearson had made select appearances at drag races driving Owens' quarter-miler, the "Cotton Picker"), and both were aching for a chance to prove what the team could do. A second at Riverside and a third in the Daytona 500 were encouraging, and Pearson's first win of the season came at Hickory in April.

He went on to win the next three races in a row. All told, Pearson won sixteen GN events that year, scored top-five berths at eleven others, and in so doing, won $78,193 and his first Grand National driving championship. Interestingly, not one of the victories that year came on a superspeedway, strange when you consider that Pearson was known as the "King of the Big Tracks" later in his career.

Pearson started 1967 driving for Cotton Owens and Dodge, but that changed after Fred Lorenzen's surprise retirement from racing, and by May, Pearson had signed with the Holman and Moody team to take Lorenzen's place. Pearson's first race in an H&M Fairlane came at the Rebel 400, where he picked up the No. 17 that he would soon make famous. Pearson won the pole with a new track record of 144.536mph, then battled all day with Richard Petty. It was the first of many such superspeedway confrontations between a Petty Mopar and a Pearson Ford or Mercury. On that particular occasion it was Petty who prevailed. It wouldn't always be so.

Pearson stayed with Holman and Moody for 1968 and campaigned a fleet of gold-over-blue, fast-backed Torinos. His crew chief that year was the recently retired Holman and Moody driver Dick Hutcherson. With Hutch's help, 1968 became Pearson's single most successful year of racing, and he started the season with a second place at Riverside. New Fomoco teammate Cale Yarborough dominated all comers at the Daytona 500 in his slippery Wood Brothers' Mercury, but after that Pearson was literally off to the races. A big win came at Darlington in the Rebel 400, but as in 1966, Pearson picked up the balance of his fifteen other wins and sixteen top-five finishes on the short tracks. Yet a win is a win, and in this case, sixteen wins in forty-seven outings won Pearson his second Grand National driving championship and (although H&M Fords had been

When the factory Aero-Wars broke out in 1969, Pearson went to war in an H&M Torino Talladega. Not even the mid-season introduction of the winged Dodge Daytona could keep him from winning his third Grand National championship. The Daytona Racing Archives

It was the Ralph Moody-inspired "beak" on Pearson's Talladega that made the car so successful. By the 1971 cessation of hostilities in the Aero-Wars, Pearson and his other Fomoco drivers had scored twenty-two superspeedway wins to just thirteen recorded by Daytona and Superbird drivers. Craft Photo

winning since 1957) the first national title for Holman and Moody.

The year of the "Aero-Wars" in NASCAR racing was 1969. When Chryco engineers cooked up a slippery new version of their fuselage-bodied Charger—called the Charger 500 for obvious reasons—Ford engineers and Ralph Moody responded with a droop-snouted aero car of their own called the Torino Talladega. Ford engineers also had another ace up their sleeve called the Blue Crescent, or Boss 429 racing Hemi. Both were waiting for the new Mopar menace when Speed Weeks 1969 dawned. Though the bosses of NASCAR put the Boss motor on hold until later in the season, Ford Talladega pilots like David Pearson and LeeRoy Yarbrough were still able to stop the new Dodges' "charge" at Daytona using the previous year's 427 Tunnel Port engines. Pearson was the fastest at Daytona that year and his Talladega scorched the tri-oval with a best speed of 190.029mph. Yarbrough won the 500 in his Junior Johnson-prepped Talladega while Pearson finished sixth. The No. 17 car's first win of 1969 came two weeks later at Rockingham in the Carolina 500, and Pearson went on to win the Yankee 600 (at Michigan) that year, but again, as in 1966 and 1969, his short track success clinched him his third Grand National driving championship. In so doing he became only the second man (after Lee Petty) to win three national driving titles.

After that season, Pearson announced that he would no longer run for the championship. He said he had achieved his goal of winning a championship ring for each of his three sons, so in the future he would only run at selected races, not the full circuit. Pearson stayed with Holman and Moody for 1970 and just missed winning the Daytona 500 when worn tires caused him to slide wide in turn four of the last lap—permitting Pete Hamilton to slip past the H&M Talladega in his Petty-prepared Superbird. Though Pearson won the Rebel 400 that year (his second of seven such wins), on the whole, 1970 was a wash for him and the rest of the Fomoco teams due to new Ford chief Lee Iacocca's decision to slash the corporate racing by a withering 75 percent.

Pearson began 1971 with the downsized Holman and Moody operation and won a Daytona qualifying race and at Bristol, but a salary dispute with John Holman led to his departure from the team after the Rebel 400 in May. For a brief period, Pearson fielded Pontiacs for the second time in his career, in this case, cars prepared by Ray Nichels.

When 1972 dawned, Pearson was without a regular ride and made a one-time appearance for Bud Moore's Ford team at the Atlanta 500. He finally found a permanent new "home" in April when the Wood Brothers gave him the nod to replace A.J. Foyt (who had decided to concentrate on Indy Car racing) in the No. 21 Purolator Cyclone. The combination was an immediate success and Pearson won the first race he ran for the team, the 1972 Rebel 400 at Darlington. Over the next seven years, Pearson and the Wood Brothers dominated the superspeedways. Their partnership produced an incredible forty-three Winston Cup victories, all but one of which came on superspeedways. Though the team only ran a limited schedule, it won just about every race it chose to enter. In 1973, for example, Pearson and his Boss 429-powered Mercury won an amazing eleven of the eighteen races they entered, and took two seconds and a third in three others. In 1976, he won ten of twenty-two events and captured NASCAR's triple crown by winning the Daytona 500, the World 600, and the Southern 500. He also won both races at Michigan along with the Atlanta 500 and the Rebel 500, an incredible performance. It was during this era that Pearson picked up his Silver Fox nickname. One of the greatest finishes in NASCAR history came in the 1976 Daytona 500 when Pearson and Richard Petty crashed on the last turn on the last lap while battling for the lead. Petty's car plowed head first into the outside wall and came to a stop on the tri-oval grass, a mere 100ft from the finish line. Pearson's red-and-white Mercury had also taken a header into the wall during the melee and came to a stop at the foot of pit road. Though stunned, Pearson still had the presence of mind to bump the car into gear and he was able to limp across the starting line before Petty could get restarted. It was to be Pearson's only Daytona 500 win.

Pearson and the Wood Brothers parted company in 1979 after a communication foul-up in the

After leaving H&M, Pearson signed on with the Wood Brothers. The Mercurys he drove for that team ruled during the superspeedways during the seventies. Craft Photo

Pearson's Holman and Moody Torinos won just about everything there was to win in '68 and '69. Here Dick Hutcherson (hands on pit wall wearing glasses), Pearson-'s H&M crew chief, oversees a stop at Riverside. Craft Collection

The exaggerated fastback roofline of the 1968 Torino made the car aerodynamically superior in Grand National trim to just about everything else on the track. David

Pearson put that aero-advantage to use during the '68 NASCAR season and was rewarded with his second national driving title. Craft Collection

Rebel 500 resulted in Pearson jetting out of the pits during the race with lug nuts on only two of his Mercury's four wheels. He got as far as the end of pit road before the car and its unsecured tires parted company in the most embarrassing way imaginable. Pearson's final two NASCAR wins came in the 1979 Southern 500 and the 1980 Rebel 500 while he was substituting for an injured Dale Earnhardt in Hoss Ellington's car.

Pearson campaigned his own WC Monte Carlo under Chattanooga Chew colors until 1986, when he shifted his attention to helping eldest son, Larry, win two Busch Grand National Championships.

Though not on the track, Pearson never admitted to retiring until 1989, when an old back problem prevented him from reuniting with the Wood Brothers at Charlotte.

Pearson is without doubt one of the greatest NASCAR drivers of all time. Yet he remains a quiet and almost painfully shy man. When asked about his incredible career, he has said, "I don't guess I take the time to look back very often. When I do it gives me a warm feeling. There were a lot more good times than there were bad, and a lot more good luck than bad, I guess." Good luck, indeed.

Lee, Richard, and Kyle Petty

U nlike today when a Winston Cup driver might continue to race until well into his fifties, during the earliest days of Grand National stock car racing, the sport was almost exclusively reserved for "young" men. Most drivers hung up their helmets shortly after their thirtieth birthday (if not considerably before) in the days when Tim Flock and Herb Thomas were leading the racing pack.

And that's why Lee Petty's legendary career is all the more remarkable. You see, the senior member of the racing Petty clan didn't buckle himself into a racing car until the extremely "advanced" age of thirty-five.

Petty's delayed entry into the racing fray can perhaps be explained by the devotion he felt for his family: wife, Elizabeth, and sons Maurice and Richard. Life in the Carolinas during the Depression was challenging at best and allowed little spare time for hobbies. Before taking up racing as his business, Petty had to put food on the family's Randelman, North Carolina, table by pursuing a variety of trades. At various times he had been a watermelon truck driver, a taxi driver, a mechanic, and even a hog farmer.

Richard Petty, complete with trademark cowboy hat and dark shades. Craft Collection

Young Lee had always enjoyed going fast in a car, but never thought to pursue that need for speed professionally until the inaugural "Strictly Stock" NASCAR race in June 1949. When Petty heard about that event in Charlotte, he borrowed a neighbor's 1946 Buick Roadmaster and drove it to the dirt track oval in Charlotte to try his luck. He qualified the car ninth in a field of thirty-three and was running well in the race until flipping the car three times on lap 105 (of 200). For that feat, Petty earned the dubious distinction of being the first man to wreck in NASCAR competition. He also collected $25 in winnings and, doubtless, the anger of the Buick's owner.

Even though Petty's first outing was somewhat less than successful, he was hooked. He soon returned to the circuit with a black 1949 Plymouth coupe that bore racing No. 42. He didn't know it at the time, but that first race car was the start of a family association with Plymouth (and later Dodge) that would continue for much of the next three decades. By the seventh race of that first NASCAR season, Petty had become a winning driver, his first victory coming at

Lee Petty was a driver in the NASCAR ranks from the first race in that series. The Daytona Racing Archives

Pittsburgh, Pennsylvania. The $1,500 purse he pocketed that day was the first of literally millions that Petty, his son, Richard, and his grandson, Kyle, would win over the next forty-five (and counting) years.

Before long, Petty, with the help of his two young sons, had become a force on the fledgling circuit. Back home in Level Cross, Petty began construction of a shop and racing dynasty that to date has produced hundreds of NASCAR victories for more than forty different drivers, and an unrivaled ten Grand National/Winston Cup championships. But perhaps we're getting a bit ahead of ourselves.

After his first season on the circuit, Petty began to turn in a string of remarkably consistent and financially rewarding performances. From 1949 to 1954, Petty never placed lower than fourth in the championship points standings. During that time he won six races and finished in the top five scores of other times.

In 1954, he captured his first of three Grand National driving titles. Big wins that year came at Daytona (where he won after Tim Flock was disqualified), and Martinsville, but it was primarily his consistency (seven wins and twenty-five top-ten finishes in thirty-four starts) that won him the points race. Over the next five seasons, Petty was again the soul of consistency and always finished near the top of the points standings, year in and year out. During that time, he

switched back and forth between Dodge and Oldsmobile racing iron.

Nineteen hundred and fifty-eight was more than just a year of consistent performances for Petty in a number of ways. That season was the first year of the GM-inspired AMA ban on factory-backed racing, and as a factory-backed Olds driver that year, Petty had decided advantage over the few Ford racers who raced as independents. He didn't have things quite as easy with his Chevrolet and Pontiac rivals since they, too, were still getting clandestine factory support. After being unable to catch Paul Goldsmith in Smokey Yunick's Pontiac at Daytona, Petty first got to kiss a pretty girl in victory lane at Concord in March. He collected similar busses six more times that season, and those smooches coupled with thirty-seven other top-ten finishes made Petty Grand National champion for a second time.

Another object of pride for Petty that season was the debut of his twenty-one-year-old son, Richard, in two 1958 Grand National races. The junior Petty's first run for the checkered flag came in September in Toronto, Canada. He drove one of Dad's spare Oldsmobiles that day under the number 142. The lanky lad qualified the car seventh but then fell out midway though the race when he had a close encounter with the retaining wall. Richard's winnings that day totaled $115 for finishing seventeenth in the nineteen-car field. Richard's second race came twenty-four hours later in Buffalo, New York, and this time his Olds carried the number 42A. Richard only qualified thirteenth for the 25mi event, but this time his car was running at the finish—albeit a full four laps down. Richard made $40 more than he had in his first NASCAR race to bring his total earnings up to $170 for the 1958 season. From such a humble beginning a "kingdom" was to grow.

In 1959, Lee Petty did what no other man had done before: win a third Grand National driving championship. Once again with Oldsmobile that year, Petty achieved a sort of immortality by winning the first Daytona 500 at Big Bill France's all-new 2.5mi temple of speed. Though Petty qualified a distant fifteenth for the inaugural 500, by lap 150 he had put his block-long '59 Olds in the lead. The next thirty-eight laps would prove to be a harbinger of the close racing for which Daytona would soon become famous. The lead changed no fewer than eleven times after Petty first put his No. 42 Olds out front. When he and Beauchamp roared across the finish line on lap 200, their cars were so close together it took 61 hours of photographic evaluation to determine who had actually won. In the end, a majority of the shots that NASCAR officials had collected from track photographers showed Petty's car ahead of Beauchamp's by the slightest of margins. The average speed for that first 500 was 135.521mph.

Son Richard also started the first 500, this time driving his 1957 Olds convertible bearing No. 43

Petty had a fondness for Chrysler race cars that had a great influence on both his racing career and that of his son Richard. The Daytona Racing Archives

from the sixth starting position on the grid. Unfortunately, by lap eight of the race he was watching the race from pit road, the victim of a blown engine. But he did show promise later in the season when he drove his white No. 43 Plymouth (he and Lee having switched back to Mopar machines at midseason) to a fourth-place finish in the Southern 500. During the rest of the season, Lee Petty scored ten more Grand National wins, the most he had ever racked up in a season.

Nineteen hundred and sixty was another solid year for father Petty on the circuit, and it was also the season when son Richard notched his first three GN wins. The first of what ultimately would be 200 NASCAR victories came for the younger Petty in a 100mi dirt track race at the Charlotte fairgrounds. In the rest of the twenty-one car field that Petty vanquished that day was another Carolinian driver named David Pearson. It would not be the last time

that the two tangled for a NASCAR win. The first "major" win of Richard Petty's career came at Martinsville in the Virginia 500. Petty qualified his 325hp Plymouth fourth behind pole sitter Glen Wood and went on to a $3,340 victory.

Lee Petty's last season of competition was 1961, though that probably wasn't his plan as he pulled into the garage area at Daytona for Speed Weeks 1961. The week got off to a bad start for the Petty family when a nudge from Junior Johnson sent Richard over the wall on lap thirty-seven of the first 100mi qualifying race. Richard suffered abrasions to both eyes and a cut hand and did not run in the 500.

As it turned out, neither did his dad. That's because later that same afternoon, the senior Petty also took an airborne trip outside the speedway, with much graver consequences. That particular wreck, on lap thirty-seven of the second qualifying race, occurred when Petty and Johnny Beauchamp tangled

Petty's crash in the Daytona 500 is still one of the most dramatic in NASCAR history. It began when his #42 Plymouth tangled with Johnny Beauchamp's Chevrolet in the banking of turn four. Craft Collection

injuries. Beauchamp was luckier and only sustained head injuries. Petty spent four months in the hospital and eventually recovered. He even returned to the track two years later, to make a brief comeback, but his racing career effectively ended just outside of turn four that day in Daytona. The fifty-four wins he scored during his time on the circuit still place him seventh on the all-time win list.

Though his dad's career had come to a crashing halt, young Richard's Grand National star was on the rise. When he returned to the fray after Daytona he scored his fourth and fifth wins later that season. Eight more wins came in 1962 and Petty showed a flash of his superspeedway greatness to come when he barely lost the Daytona 500 to Fireball Roberts and his Smokey Yunick-prepared Pontiac. Nineteen hundred and sixty-three was Petty's best year yet and he won fourteen more races toward his ultimate 200. He finished second only to Joe Weatherly in the points race that year and came back the following year to win his first GN championship.

In 1964, Mopar drivers like Petty got their first taste of 426 Hemi power. Though that engine had been purpose-built for stock car racing and would not appear in a regular production automobile for two more years, the sanctioning gods deemed it "stock." Ford drivers didn't have much of a chance against the new Hemi-headed mill, even though their Galaxies had received a set of "High Riser" cylinder heads that were also hardly "production" items. They were understandably upset by the presence of the new Mopar motors along pit road and voiced their unhappiness. Their howls of protest grew even

as they entered turn four. The two cars went out of control at more than 150mph, then scaled the retaining barrier at the top of the 33-degree banked turn. When that happened there was nothing but blue sky below both cars until they came crashing to earth several stories below. Both cars were totally demolished, Petty's landing so far outside the track it was almost in the parking lot just beyond the turn. He was seriously injured and suffered a punctured lung, multiple fractures of the left chest, a fractured left thigh, a broken collarbone, and multiple internal

In the blink of an eye, both cars became airborne and vaulted completely outside of the track. Craft Collection

Petty's Plymouth landed in a crumpled heap outside the banking of turn four and nearly in the spectator parking area. Though badly injured, Petty did survive, but his racing career was effectively over. Craft Collection

louder after the Daytona 500, where Petty's electric blue Belvedere lead a three-car Plymouth sweep of the top finishing positions. It was the first of a phenomenal seven Daytona 500 wins for Petty, and coupled with eight other firsts and twenty-six top-five finishes, it helped make him the 1964 Grand National driving champion.

By the end of the season, Ford's noisy complaints about the 426 Hemi's legality led NASCAR to reverse itself and declare the engine verboten. Though the sanctioning body also outlawed Ford's suspect "High Riser" head castings, Dodge and Plymouth racers were little appeased. They ultimately chose to boycott the 1965 season altogether.

Petty spent his time off from NASCAR campaigning a Petty Blue Barracuda drag race car called the 43 Jr. He and the Mopar legions came back in 1966 when NASCAR once again allowed the now-regular

production Hemi engine to compete. When NASCAR would not let Ford racers campaign their 427 single overhead cam engine, it was Ford's turn to walk out of the series. As a result, it was a very good year for Mopar drivers like Petty, as he added eight more notches to his winner's "belt" in 1966, including his first superspeedway wins at both Atlanta and Darlington.

As impressive as Petty's performance had been in the years preceding, it's likely that not even he was ready for the success that awaited him in 1967. In that forty-nine-race season on the Grand National circuit, he forever earned the crown of "King" of stock car racing. And even today, Petty still doesn't know exactly how it all came about. After all, the car he used that season was unchanged from the one he campaigned the year before. Ditto for the engine. His archrival Fords were no longer on the sidelines,

Lee's eldest son, Richard, started his NASCAR career in the late fifties driving Dad's "old" race cars. Craft Collection

having returned in late 1966 with a fleet of (you guessed it) decidedly nonproduction 427 Tunnel Port-headed engines that breathed nearly as well as the Hemi. But even having said all of that, 1967 was Richard Petty's year in stock car racing.

Win number one came at Weaverville in a short track race, and before the year was over he had visited victory lane twenty-six more times. At one point during the season, the rest of the field should have just stayed home as Petty won an incredible ten races in a row, including his first victory in the Southern 500. It's highly unlikely that anyone will ever break the single-season record for wins Petty set in 1967. As you might have guessed, Petty picked up his second GN championship that year.

The King suffered a reversal of sorts in 1968 when Fomoco unveiled two all-new Ford and Mercury intermediate body styles that featured wind-cheating fastback rooflines. Suddenly Cale Yarborough, LeeRoy Yarbrough, and David Pearson were the kings of the superspeedways, not Petty—or any

By the mid-sixties, Richard was a NASCAR star in his own right. He drove this Plymouth to the '67 championship. Along the way he was "crowned" King of stock car racing. The Daytona Racing Archives

This was Petty's "throne" in 1967. The races he won while seated here made him the king of stock car racing. Craft Photo

other Mopar racer, for that matter. Making things worse for Petty at Daytona that year was the vinyl roof on his Road Runner that became something of a parachute when debris broke the car's windshield. Though he won sixteen races that season, he finished third in the points chase.

Due to their poor showing on the superspeedways in 1968, Dodge engineers burned tankersful of midnight oil trying to counter the aerodynamic advantage the new Fomoco intermediates enjoyed over the new-for-1968 Charger. Their eventual solution was to fare over the car's tunneled-in back light and to bring the grille flush with the surrounding bodywork. The new, special-bodied car was called the Dodge Charger 500 for obvious reasons. Unfortunately for Plymouth drivers, the Mayflower division had no plans to make similar changes to the Satellite body styles that they drove. When Richard Petty got wind of the new Dodges, he immediately asked his corporate sponsors to let him switch to Dodge for 1969. In what has to be one of the most obtuse corporate decisions made during the factory-backed NASCAR wars, the answer Petty got was a flat *no*.

Knowing when to take no for an answer, Petty wasted little time in calling Ford racing Czar Jacque Passino to see if the offers Passino had been making for the past several seasons were still good. When the answer Petty got to that question was a resounding *yes*, he broke Mopar lover's hearts everywhere by signing on with Ford's 1969 "going thing." That meant that Petty would be campaigning a special

Petty jumped ship to campaign a Ford Talladega in 1969. He won ten races that year while breaking Mopar fans' hearts. The Daytona Racing Archives

Big money and a winged Road Runner brought Petty back to Mopar in 1970. Here he dukes it out with LeeRoy Yarbrough's Torino Talladega. Craft Collection

aero-bodied car after all. In this case, a droop-snouted Ford Torino Talladega—Ford's answer to the Charger 500.

And better yet, 1969 was also the year that Ford finally got NASCAR to sign off on a race-legal Fomoco racing Hemi, the Boss 429. Petty signaled his comfort with his new Torino surroundings by winning the first race of the 1969 season at Riverside, which was also the first roadrace victory of his career. The Talladega proved to be a far superior car to the Charger 500, and Chryco engineers had to go back to the drawing board once again.

This time they hurriedly grafted on a pointy snout and soaring rear wing. The result was the Charger Daytona. In 1969, it didn't make much difference, and the new winged car was unable to slow the Fomoco aero-juggernaut. Talladega drivers like Petty and their counterparts in Spoiler II's (Mercury's version of the big T) won thirty of the fifty-four races that season. Incredibly, though Petty and his crew had absolutely no Ford experience going into the season, they won ten times and finished the season second in points only to Holman and Moody Talladega pilot David Pearson.

Plymouth was smarting from Petty's defection to Ford all season long. Something had to be done to

get the "King" back, and money wasn't going to be enough to do the job. So, taking a page from the Dodge boy's book, Plymouth engineers pasted on a pointy beak and soaring rear wing to transform their aerodynamic ugly duckling Satellite into a sleek, wind-cheating Superbird.

With the new Mopar-winged car, coupled with Chryco's promise to make Petty Engineering the Plymouth and Dodge version of Ford's Holman and Moody (read: buckets of greenbacks), Petty decided that one season with Ford was quite enough. It could just be that Ford's 1969 decision to cut its 1970 racing budget by 75 percent had a little bit to do with the King's return to Plymouth. For whatever reason, it was an exceedingly good decision.

When the warm Florida sun dawned on Speed Weeks 1970, Petty Engineering was in Daytona with not one but two new Petty Blue Superbirds. Petty's car carried his traditional No. 43 while newcomer Pete Hamilton's was dressed in No. 40 livery. Petty ultimately blew an engine in the 500, but Hamilton was there to pick up the slack. When race leader David Pearson's Talladega momentarily lost traction in turn four of the last lap, Hamilton slipped by to take his first and only 500 win. With the Fomoco teams crippled by the decreased flow of factory dol-

Petty's personal favorite race cars were the Coke bottle-bodied Chargers he drove in the mid-seventies. Craft Photo

When his Dodges were no longer competitive, Petty switched to GM and, eventually, drove #43 Pontiacs through the last seasons of his driving career. Craft Collection

Petty prepared his Ford, Mopar, and GM race cars at a shop right next to his dad Lee's house in Level Cross, North Carolina. Craft Photo

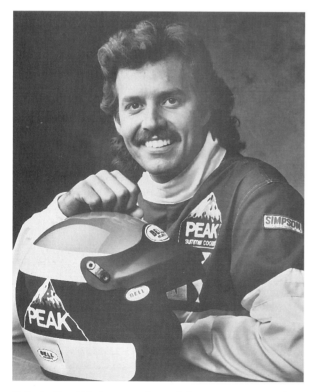

Kyle is the third generation of Pettys to venture into NASCAR racing. Craft Collection

lars, Superbird and Daytona drivers had a romp. Petty himself picked up eighteen more GN wins.

The Aero-Wars were over in 1971 and the NASCAR rule book was the winner. Alarmed by the 200mph velocities the special body cars were capable of, the sanctioning body had introduced restrictor plates during the 1970 season and outlawed the special sheet metal altogether for 1971. When that happened, King Richard campaigned a boxy '71 Road Runner. Though clumsy looking, it proved to be one of his most successful race cars. In fact, it earned him twenty-one more wins and his third national championship. In 1972, that same Road Runner body style was the first Petty car to carry his new red-and-blue STP racing livery. Near the end of the season Petty switched those colors to a swoopy Charger body style that he would campaign for the next five years.

Today Petty names those Coke bottle-bodied Dodges as his favorite racing cars. And that's not surprising since they helped him win thirty-eight more Winston cup races, three more NASCAR championships, and nearly $1.5 million in prize money.

When the Charger body style was finally declared illegal for Winston Cup competition, Petty, ever the Mopar loyalist, fought on with a new Dodge Magnum. It was not a lovely car either on and off the track, and Petty's 1978 season was a

Since starting on the tour, Kyle has driven both Fords and Pontiacs. Craft Collection

disaster; he won no races that season, so he switched to General Motors for 1979. It was a smart move and resulted in his seventh and final Winston Cup championship. Petty ran the balance of his illustrious career in Oldsmobiles and Pontiacs. And it was, of course, while mounted in an STP No. 43 Pontiac that Petty won his 200th NASCAR race in Daytona at the 1984 Firecracker 400. Win number 201 never came (it would have spoiled the symmetry anyway), and Petty retired from NASCAR at the close of the 1993 season. He is simply the greatest driver in NASCAR history. Today he oversees the operation of the STP racing team, so King Richard will still be a fixture in the Winston Cup garage area for years to come.

Richard Petty's retirement from the ranks of active drivers has not meant the disappearance of the Petty name from the winner's column on the Winston Cup circuit. That's because since 1979 his son, Kyle, has followed in father Richard's oh-so-large (and rapid) footsteps. The first race for the third generation of racing Pettys came at Daytona in 1979, when the eighteen-year-old Kyle drove one of his dad's leftover Magnums to victory in the ARCA race during Speed Weeks. Shortly thereafter, Kyle began to make selected appearances on the regular Winston Cup circuit. The first of those came at Talladega in August at the Talladega 500. Still driving a Mag-

num, Kyle qualified eighteenth for the superspeedway event and finished a very creditable ninth.

By 1981, Kyle was running the full Winston Cup tour in the Petty Enterprises team car. He stayed with the family team through the 1984 season and recorded four top-five finishes in 139 starts. In 1985, Kyle signed to drive Ford Thunderbirds for the fabled Wood Brothers team. While driving their Ford, Petty became the first third-generation driver to win a NASCAR stock car race. The first win for the youngest Petty came in 1986 at Richmond, when he won the Miller High Life 400 (formerly the Richmond 400). Nineteen hundred and eighty-seven produced another win for Kyle and the Woods, this one coming on Memorial Day weekend at the World 600 in Charlotte.

In 1989, Petty left the Wood Brothers and Ford for a Pontiac Grand Prix fielded by Felix Sabates. It's been a successful pairing and the pair has won four races and placed in the top ten twenty-three times since becoming a team. At just thirty-four years of age, it's likely that Kyle will remain a Winston Cup regular for many years to come, especially now that he's given up the idea of a country music singing career in favor of focusing all his efforts on racing. And it's even possible that one of his three young sons may one day grow up to be the fourth generation of Pettys to win in NASCAR competition.

CHAPTER 17

Fireball Roberts

At first blush, Edward Glenn Roberts, Jr., would seem to have been a thoroughly unlikely candidate to become Grand National stock car racing's first nationally feted superstar driver. Born in Tavares, Florida, far from the moonshining tradition and dirt track bull rings of the Carolinas, Roberts had played varsity baseball for his Apopka High School and local American Legion teams (earning him the nickname "Fireball" for his blistering fast pitching) before going on to pursue an undergraduate degree at the University of Florida (UF) in Gainesville. Chances are that Fireball might have pursued a career in professional baseball had it not been for his family's move to Daytona Beach in 1945. Then, as now, Daytona was the center for automotive competition, so perhaps it's only natural that Fireball would retire his fastball for an even more rapid form of competition.

When the first stock car beach race was held on Daytona's hard-packed silver sands in 1948, Roberts was among the drivers in the field. Though a ninth lap shunt put him out of

Fireball was one of the early standouts in NASCAR racing and that sport's first superstar. The Daytona Racing Archives

the running early in the event, more starts on the fledgling circuit soon followed. Ultimately, Fireball's pursuit of racing success led to his withdrawal from mechanical engineering studies at UF. After two years and a semester of college, Roberts decided that his place was on the track and not in the classroom. Stock car racing would never be the same. Roberts' first win in Grand National (nee Winston Cup) competition came in 1950 in Hillsboro, North Carolina. Just twenty-one years old at the time, Fireball dominated that 100mi affair and showed his back bumper to such leading lights as Curtis Turner, Lee Petty, Herb Thomas, and Marshall Teague on his way to victory lane.

Roberts' victory made him the youngest winner on the circuit (indeed, even today, nearly fifty years later, only one driver younger than Fireball was at the time has ever found victory lane in NASCAR's big leagues). Far from being a fluke, Fireball underscored that first triumph with a solid second-place finish at the inaugural running of the Southern 500 in Darlington just one month later. It

In 1962, Fireball drove to victory in the Daytona 500 just ahead of Richard Petty. Craft Collection

was clear that his star was on the rise. When his first full season of competition was over, he was second only to Grand National champion Bill Rexford in the season's points chase.

Fireball's ascent to superstar status began in 1956 when he signed on as a driver for former Indy 500 winner Pete DePaolo's West Coast-based operation. By the mid-fifties, NASCAR had grown beyond its rural southeastern roots to the point that most of the major automobile manufacturers had come to covet the publicity that Grand National victories could garner. When the Ford Motor Company decided to pursue sales-generating NASCAR wins in earnest, DePaolo was the man they chose to get the job done. Other members of DePaolo's Ford-backed team included Curtis Turner, Joe Weatherly, Ralph Moody, Marvin Panch, and Louis "Red" Vogt.

That year at Daytona, Fireball's cars first picked up the No. 22 racing livery associated with him for most of the rest of his career. At season's end Fireball had visited GN victory lane five times. When Ralph Moody and John Holman's new racing partnership became Ford's factory-backed racing outlet, Fireball stayed at the helm of a No. 22, Blue Oval-powered car and brought Holman and Moody several of that soon-to-be-famous racing "factory's" early victories. One of the more notable of those was Fireball's triumph at the first Rebel 400 (then a convertible class race) at Darlington. That early success coupled with

subsequent wins at the always cantankerous "Lady in Black" no doubt played a part in Fireball's claim that Darlington was his favorite track.

Fireball campaigned a Ford for 1957, first as part of the factory effort and later that season as an independent car owner after the Automobile Manufacturers of America "ban" on factory-backed motorsports competition. That spurred a mechanical change of allegiance for Fireball, who opened the 1958 season behind the wheel of a '57 Chevrolet. As it turned out, 1958 was the year that Fireball's on-track success brought him to national prominence. When that fifty-race season ended, Fireball had recorded six wins (five of them won back-to-back) in just ten starts and had pocketed $32,218—more money than any other driver on the circuit. Fireball was selected as the 1958 professional athlete of the year by the Florida Sportswriters Association, an honor previously only bestowed on "stick-and-ball" types. It's been said that Fireball was prouder of that award than any other he received in his career.

In 1959, Fireball began what turned out to be a four-year association with legendary mechanic Henry "Smokey" Yunick and Pontiac. Like Chevrolet, Pontiac's racing was little impeded by the erstwhile AMA ban and the backdoor of its high-performance parts division was always open wide to Yunick and other "Poncho" racers. That semi-official factory support, coupled with Yunick's genius at flexibly interpreting the NASCAR rules book, could almost guarantee suc-

Fireball's 500-winning car was built by legendary mechanic Smokey Yunick. Craft Photo

Stock cars really were pretty stock in 1962. Note the factory dash, seat, and roll-up windows in Fireball's '62 Catalina. Craft Photo

cess for even a mediocre driver, let alone one with Fireball's proven ability. So it came as no surprise that Roberts was soon parking his black-and-gold No. 22 Catalinas in victory lane. Nineteen hundred and sixty-two was undoubtedly the year of greatest success for the Roberts/Yunick partnership, even though that duo parted ways at midseason. Fireball won the pole for the Daytona 500 that year, was the top qualifier for the third year in a row, and won one of the traditional 100mi (now 125mi) qualifying heats. In the 500 itself, Roberts charged into the lead and led 144 of the race's 200 laps to take the win. Pictures of Roberts sharing a victory lane kiss with former Miss America Mary Ann Mobley graced sports pages all across America the next day.

Unfortunately, all was not well within the team, and later that season Yunick and Roberts parted ways. When Roberts left Smokey's "Best Damn Garage in Town" he took with him one of the '62 Super Duty Catalinas Smokey had built, and with the mechanical backing of Banjo Matthews, he competed at selected events for the balance of the season. One of those was the 1962 running of the Fourth of July Firecracker classic, where Fireball completed his dominance at Daytona that year by once again driving home in first place.

When not turning left on the NASCAR circuit in 1962, Fireball spent time on the sports car and world endurance racing circuits, where he campaigned a Ferrari at the 24 Hours of Le Mans and several other road course events.

Roberts found himself driving a Pontiac Grand National car again in 1963—until GM decided to truly close up its racing operations out of fear that continued high-profile success might bring federal antitrust litigation. Fortunately for Fireball, Ford decided to get back into racing in a big way and Holman and Moody once again headed up the corporation's NASCAR program. One Ford goal was to sign as many of NASCAR's top drivers as possible to Ford contracts. Racing chief Jacque Passino pulled out all the stops in his pursuit of Roberts, and by the thirteenth race of the 1963 season (at Bristol in March), Roberts was driving a "Passino Purple" No. 22 Ford Galaxie. Fireball led 163 of the race's 500 laps on his way to taking the checkered flag. Later that year, Fireball parked his 427-powered Ford in Daytona's victory lane after sling-shotting past teammate Fred Lorenzen's Galaxie on the last lap of the Firecracker 400. Two months later Fireball again dominated the field at the Southern 500 on his way to a fourth win at Darlington. At season's end Fireball was fifth in points and had pocketed more winnings than every other driver, save for Fred Lorenzen and season champion Joe Weatherly.

Unfortunately, Fireball was not able to build on that success the following season. A top-five finish at Riverside was marred by Joe Weatherly's midrace death, and mechanical failure spoiled Fireball's

Fireball got to kiss former Miss America Mary Ann Mobley (left) in Daytona's victory lane in 1962. The Daytona Racing Archives

chances for a second Daytona 500 win. Though he took second in several races following Daytona, the May running of the World 600 still found Roberts without a win, and rumors suggested that he would soon hang up his helmet in favor of a job as spokesman for a national brewing company. Unfortunately, to the horror of the Memorial Day crowd at Charlotte, Fireball got caught up in a shunt caused by Ned Jarrett and Junior Johnson that resulted in horrible burns over most of his body. Though Jarrett rushed to Fireball's aid before the flames were able to take Fireball's life at the scene, it was already too late. By late June complications set in and Fireball, just thirty-five years old, passed away on July 2 at a hospital in Charlotte. Fittingly, Fireball was buried in a quiet cemetery just a few blocks east of the Daytona International Speedway.

Though he's been gone from the racing scene for more than three decades, Fireball Roberts still ranks sixth on the all-time list for superspeedway poles, and his thirty-two Grand National victories still place him fifteenth on the all-time win list. After Fireball's death, Smokey Yunick said that intelligence was Fireball's major competitive weapon. "He planned each race carefully. He didn't play it by ear. He went over each race lap-by-lap and studied every other driver carefully. . . . He rated them under various track conditions so he knew how much exposure he could risk to himself and his car."

Ned Jarrett, later a Grand National driving champion, called Fireball "the most respected driver there ever was." Richard Petty, a rising star at the time of Roberts' death, claimed that Fireball "helped the sport more than anybody."

Fireball Roberts' last year in NASCAR racing was 1964. His competitive mount that year was a metallic purple Holman and Moody Galaxie. Unfortunately it was in one *of those competition-proven cars that he was mortally burned in the World 600.* PPG Archives

In 1963, Fireball signed with Ford and Holman and Moody. His "Passino Purple" Galaxies were much feared. Unfortunately, a wreck in 1964 claimed his life. The Daytona Racing Archives

Some contend that Fireball was the greatest stock car driver of all time. And while that is a ques-Some contend that Fireball was the greatest stock car driver of all time. And while that is a question that can never be accurately answered, it is certain that his accomplishments on the NASCAR circuit during the fifties and sixties played a fundamental role in making stock car racing the nationally respected sport that it is today.

CHAPTER 18

Herb Thomas

"If they can do that, so can I," is what Herbert Watson Thomas said the first time that he and a group of friends attended an unsanctioned "hot rod" race in Greensboro, North Carolina, just after World War II. And right he was. One year later, when the National Association for Stock Car Automobile Racing (NASCAR) was organized, Herb Thomas was one of the first drivers to sign up for the new series. During the first few years of that fledgling series, Thomas was the man to beat. Though his career lasted just six short years, Thomas managed to win an incredible forty-eight Grand National events, a mark that still places him tenth on NASCAR's all-time winners' list more than thirty years after his last lap around a track.

Born on April 6, 1923, Thomas was the first of five sons in a family that had no connection to auto racing whatsoever. Though a native North Carolinian, Thomas spent his formative years working on the family farm and at a sawmill his father owned in Barbecue Township, North Carolina, rather than running "shine" like so many of his con-

Later, he campaigned Chrysler 300s and Chevrolets. The Daytona Racing Archives

temporaries. Thomas stayed on at the lumber mill during World War II and married his high school sweetheart, Helen, in 1941. Children came quickly and he and his wife already had two sons before Herb ever saw his first automobile race. So it no doubt came as something of a surprise to Mrs. Thomas when the quiet country boy decided to take up the pastime of Grand National stock car racing. According to Thomas today, his involvement in the sport began as little more than a hobby that he participated in when business and farm concerns permitted. But by the time Big Bill France organized NASCAR and began to sanction formal races in 1949, Thomas had come to look upon the sport as a livelihood. And well he should have. Thomas was a natural race car driver even without a shine-running apprenticeship, and he began to win races almost as soon as he showed up on the circuit.

When the first "strictly stock" (the original name for NASCAR's Grand National division, which is now called Winston Cup) was held at the Charlotte Speedway in June 1949,

NASCAR racing at Daytona 1950. Note the absence of anything resembling high banks. Craft Collection

Thomas' 1947 Ford was in the field. Unfortunately, spring failure sidelined the car and produced a non-paying twenty-ninth-place finish. Thomas picked up his first NASCAR prize money at the second GN race when his '49 Ford came home twelvth in the first Daytona Beach race sanctioned by France's organization. Thomas' earnings that day totaled $50 (not all that bad when you consider that the race winner Red Byron only pocketed $2,000). Thomas snared his first Grand National win a bit more than a year later at Martinsville, Virginia, when he outpaced Lee Petty in a 100mi dirt track race in October 1950. Thomas' first few wins came in lightweight Plymouth business coupes, but fellow driver Marshall Teague soon talked Thomas into switching to Hudson Hornets. Hudson was one of the first domestic manufacturers to see the publicity and sales benefits of NASCAR victories, and thus was one of the first carmakers to funnel sponsorship and technical aid to drivers.

Thomas' first outing in a "Fabulous Hudson" came at the second annual running of the Southern 500 in Darlington. Driving a car borrowed from Teague, Thomas qualified his No. 92 Hudson second. He started alongside Teague, who earned the Southern 500 pole in his own Hudson with an 87.636mph hot lap during qualifying. After an early series of lead changes, Thomas and his Hudson went on to lead all

but ninety of the 400 laps raced, including the last 305 circuits of the track. Thomas' victory was the first of three Southern 500 wins he would score during the next five years. For the season, Thomas' seven wins earned him the 1951 Grand National championship and his $21,050 in prize money put him atop the prize money standings.

Thomas was back in a Hudson in 1952 and was once again the man to beat. Though he had eight victories, Thomas was edged out of a second consecutive championship by Tim Flock, who also had eight wins for Hudson that season. Things were different for 1953 as Thomas' Hudson won just about everything—twelve races in all—including his second Grand National driving championship.

Though Thomas drove his own machines for most of his career, he teamed up with Smokey Yunick in 1954 and won twelve more races for Hudson, including his second Southern 500, then the most coveted victory on the circuit. Though he had won more races and money than any other driver on the circuit, Thomas was denied a third GN title by Chrysler driver Lee Petty, who amassed almost 300 more points than Thomas.

Hudson enjoyed its last NASCAR success in 1955. Though a Hornet's flathead six engine had been just the ticket for mastering the dirt tracks of the era, by

Herb Thomas gained first driving fame at the wheel of Fabulous Hudson Hornets. Craft Photo

1955 there were fewer and fewer dirt track races. The big three auto makers were also making mechanical advances daily and the move was on to overhead valves. Thomas began 1955 with a win for Hudson at West Palm Beach, but it would be Hudson's final Grand National victory; in April he and Yunick switched to General Motors cars. In September, Thomas and Yunick took a new small-block-powered Chevrolet to the Southern 500 in Darlington. Still recovering from a broken leg he had suffered four months earlier, Thomas had promised while still in the hospital that he would "bag" his third Southern 500 win. Few at the time took that boast seriously. The cars to beat for 1954 were the Hemi-powered Chrysler 300s campaigned by Tim and Fonty Flock; the races they didn't dominate were won by drivers such as Buck Baker and Junior Johnson in new overhead-valve-engined Oldsmobile Rocket 88s. Chevrolet's diminutive new '55 Chevrolets were powered by equally unimposing 265ci engines, and were unknown quantities. But they were light, and that translated into better tire wear than the heavier Chryslers (in particular) were capable of. Then there was wily old Smokey Yunick's secret weapon—a set of Firestone SuperSport tires that had been specially designed for sports car racing. Smokey's plan was to run a consistent if not blistering pace that would al-

low Thomas to take the lead and hold it when the competition was forced to come into the pits for new rubber.

When race day dawned, Darlington was a seething mass of humanity jammed to the rafters with its first sell-out crowd. The intense manufacturer's rivalry that had sprung up in the sport had aroused more spectator interest than anyone, save for Bill France, could have predicted. Thomas started eighth that day and was not a factor in the early going. In fact, it wasn't until lap 279 (of the event's 366) that Thomas and his 210 first nosed into the lead. For a while it seemed that Joe Weatherly's Holman and Moody Ford would prevail, but a collapsed wheel (and resulting wreck) finally cleared the way for Thomas' third Southern triumph. Yunick's plan had paid off and Thomas did not have to change a single tire all day. Though not apparent at the time, Thomas' win was the first of many superspeedway wins for a Bow Tie-powered car in the Grand National ranks. In many ways the Chevrolet small-block engines that drivers like Dale Earnhardt rely on today are little changed from the 265 V-8 that Thomas used to win in Darlington back in 1955.

Thomas started 1956, his last full season on the circuit, once again paired with Smokey Yunick. Ten races and two more Chevrolet victories into the sea-

Herb Thomas scored Chevrolet's first superspeedway win when he drove Smokey Yunick's car to victory at the Southern 500. The Daytona Racing Archives

son, Thomas left Yunick for Carl Kiekhaefer's all-conquering Mercury Outboards, Chrysler 300 team. And what a team it was. Paired with Tim Flock, Fonty Flock, Buck Baker, and Speedy Thompson, Thomas was part of the first truly professional NASCAR team. Kiekhaefer was a rich man and spared no expense in his pursuit of race wins. Team race cars were transported between races in semitrailer trucks (while most drivers of the day were using open trailers or actually drove their cars to the track on surface streets!), and Kiekhaefer even paid experts to consult on the weather and dirt conditions. The downside for drivers was the military discipline that Kiekhaefer demanded from his employees. Entire motels would be rented to house the team before a race, and strict curfews were followed, along with the discouragement of conjugal relations the night before a race. Kiekhaefer expected his drivers to win. And win they did in 1956. They won thirty of the fifty-six races held that year, and at one point his Chrysler 300s scored sixteen straight victories. Thomas signed on at Langhorne in April 1956 and ultimately accounted for three of those wins before he opted to campaign his own 1956 Chevrolet in July.

Those wins, coupled with his performance for Yunick and his own consistent late-season finishes, seemed to have Thomas on track for his third Grand National drivers' title. Unfortunately, a horrific wreck on the 109th lap of a dirt track event left Thomas partially paralyzed and on the sidelines for the rest of the season. It would ultimately take three long years for him to regain the full use of his right arm. Though Thomas attempted a number of comeback attempts both as a driver and car owner, he never recaptured the incredible winning form he displayed during the first half dozen years of NASCAR competition. His last race was in April of 1962, and though he was just forty years old at the time, he knew his time as a driver had come to an end. Of the 233 races Thomas started in Grand National competition, he won forty-eight, finished second or third in forty-four more, and sat on the pole thirty-nine times. His career earnings totaled $126,570—in 1950s dollars. Despite retiring from racing before many of the sport's current superstars were born, Herb Thomas is still remembered as one of the best drivers to ever take the green flag.

Chapter 19

Curtis Turner

It's safe to say that the NASCAR garage area has changed radically since the early days of the sport. Today, button-down, Brooks Brothers types are just about as common there as team mechanics, and Fortune 500 company insignia now adorn sheet metal that was once reserved exclusively for factory and dealer logos. While the infusion of "big money" into the sport has, on the whole, been a good thing, it also tended to have a homogenizing effect on the personalities that make up a racing grid. As a result, many (if not all) modern NASCAR drivers and team owners often seem to have popped out of the same well-polished mold. While nonoffending blandness may be just the ticket these days for securing and keeping a team parking space in the garage area of a NASCAR race, things weren't always that way on the circuit. Not by a long shot.

Take for example Curtis Morton Turner, easily one of the least bland, most controversial drivers to ever campaign a race car in any form of motorsports. Born in 1924 in the Shenandoah mountains, young Curtis first sustained himself with manual labor in the lumber mills in and around Floyd, Virginia. Working in the heavily

Curtis Turner had reckless good looks and an uncanny ability to drive a race car. That combination made him a standout during NASCAR's earliest days. Here, Turner (right) shakes hands with Speedy Thompson while Big Bill France (left) looks on. The Daytona Racing Archives

forested areas of the southland during the dark days of the Depression also put Turner in close contact with free-thinking souls who made their living under the moon and stars while tending to the workings of a moonshine still. Turner himself claimed that he hauled his first load of white lightning at the age of nine, and in time, the expedition required of such nocturnal automotive deliveries made the youngster the master of just about anything with four wheels. Working by day in the mills and by night on the darkened back roads of rural Virginia provided Turner with the capital to set himself up in business, and before the age of twenty he owned several sawmills plus the logging equipment and truck line necessary to keep them running.

Like other shine runners, Turner sometimes took part in word-of-mouth competitions with other drivers just for fun. As is well known by now, it was just such informal races that formed the basis for what we now know as Winston Cup Stock car racing. After a World War II stint in the Navy, Turner became more heavily involved in the fledgling sport and he soon developed a reputation for fearless close-quarter competitive-

Turner was a star on NASCAR's convertible circuit. He was also one of Holman and Moody's first team drivers. Craft Photo

often that not simply slam into the car's sheet metal until his progress was no longer impeded. Such antics quickly made Turner stand out on the barnstorming circuit (where he often rubbed fenders with drivers like the Flock brothers, Bill France, Sr., Herb Thomas, and Buck Baker). They also earned him the nickname "Pops" in honor of his fondness for "popping" a competitor's car clean off the track.

When Big Bill France brought organization to the informal bull ring races of the forties with his National Association for Stock Car Automobile Racing (NASCAR), Turner was one of the new series' earliest heroes, a fact underscored by *Sports Illustrated*'s highly unusual decision (at the time) to feature Turner in a NASCAR-related article that labeled him the "Babe Ruth" of stock car racing.

Turner's first official stock car win (unfortunately, his shine-runner victories and bull ring wins prior to NASCAR's formation will never be able to be tabulated) came at the fabled circle-shaped dirt track in Langhorne, Pennsylvania, in September 1949. One mile in circumference and "paved" with hard-packed dirt, the old Langhorne speedway was one of the most difficult and dangerous in the country. Yet Turner and his '49 Olds mastered it with ease, led all of the last fifty laps, and finished first to win the

ness. Turner's driving style was characterized by wild, dirt track broad slides on the ragged edge of control, and a quick-tempered impatience with any car ahead that wouldn't move out of the way. When his presence in the offending driver's rear view mirror wasn't enough to clear the racing line, Turner would more

Here's Turner in his '57 Holman and Moody car negotiating the famed beach course in Daytona. The Daytona Racing Archives

Believe it or not, Turner's Ford was supercharged in the '57 season. Craft Photo

Turner's fondness for bumping drivers out of his way (like Dale Earnhardt today) earned him the nickname Pops. Turner's car is shown here at Darlington in 1958 next to his close friend Joe Weatherly's Ford. That's Ralph Moody leaning on Little Joe's front fender. The Daytona Racing Archives

$2,250 purse. More wins followed in quick succession and along the way Turner also sat on the pole at the inaugural running of the Southern 500 at Darlington.

Off the track Turner had the reputation as both a savvy businessman and a hard-drinking hell raiser. When he and his lumber industry partners signed a contract worth more than $1 millon in business, a writer of the day quickly tagged Turner the "millionaire" race car driver. Though he was far from being a millionaire, Turner still enjoyed the label and often played the role to the hilt. He also equally enjoyed throwing parties for hundreds of people at a time on the spur of the moment. He was especially fond of taking dares and risks that would have trimmed years off the lives of lesser men. This was especially true where Turner's longtime friend and frequent "co-conspirator" Joe Weatherly was concerned.

Take for example the "rental car races" that Turner and Little Joe were known to engage in from time to time. According to NASCAR lore, more than a few rental cars were literally beaten to death by that duo and other drivers during impromptu midnight contests that sometimes involved racing in reverse at near triple-digit velocities from one town to the next and back again.

It's been said that many of the antics attributed to fictional driver Stroker Ace in Bill Neely's hysterical novel *Stand On It* (later made into a not-so-funny Burt Reynolds movie), are actually just thinly disguised accounts of real life Turner/Weatherly shenanigans. Other examples of Turner's reckless, devil-may-care lifestyle include the time he promised

to—and did—roll a race car over in front of Betty Skelton (famed aviatrix and early "test driver" in a number of NASCAR promotional events) during a Daytona beach course race, and the dozens of stories (perhaps only some of which were apocryphal) about the way he piloted his private plane.

There were the reports that Turner would often climb his twin-engined plane to altitude, switch on the auto pilot, place a wind-up alarm clock on the dash and fall fast asleep—much to the consternation of the passengers flying with him. Perhaps the classic Curtis Turner flying story involves the time that he and a fellow flyer were overcome with a sudden thirst for certain distilled spirits while in the air. They decided to land on a surface street in Easley, South Carolina, in order to secure the desired beverages. On the following takeoff, Turner was forced to hop-scotch several Easley motorists and ultimately became airborne only after snagging several telephone lines and the odd traffic light or two. Unlike other stories about Turner's élan for flying, this particular episode is thoroughly documented by the FAA papers that subsequently took his pilot's license away for an extended period. That grounding was no doubt made all the more bothersome for Turner by the fact that his auto driving license was oft times also held in suspension by the government for similar examples of more terrestrial liberties being taken with the law.

Turner also ran afoul of Big Bill France's "law" from time to time, too. The most notable (and for Turner, destructive) of these run-ins involved Turner's attempt to organize NASCAR's star drivers under

Turner drove a Thunderbird in the first Daytona 500 in 1959. Bill France brought his high banks days to a halt two years later when he banned Turner because of at-tempts to unionize the drivers. The Daytona Racing Archives

France lifted the lifetime ban in 1966 and Turner returned to the tour in 1967. He drove Smokey Yunick's black-and-gold Chevrolet. The Daytona Racing Archives

the Teamsters Union in 1961. Turner's work as a labor organizer came as a direct result of his partnership in the construction of the Charlotte Motor Speedway in 1959. Taking a page from Bill France's book, Turner decided to build a Daytona-like superspeedway of his own just north of Charlotte, North Carolina. When construction costs and preliminary race revenues failed to meet expectations, Turner approached the Teamsters in search of a loan. He was told that the $800,000 he needed to prop up the speedway would only be forthcoming if he agreed to organize the drivers. At first, at least, that effort at unionization met with success. In fact, Turner and fellow star driver Tim Flock were successful in signing many of the series' top drivers—until Bill France delivered a pistol-packing ultimatum that no unionized drivers would ever race on a NASCAR-sanctioned track. France's strong anti-union stand broke the back of Turner's organizing efforts and, adding insult to injury, Turner and Flock were ultimately banned from NASCAR for life.

Turner lost his Holman and Moody factory-backed ride as a direct result of his banishment, yet Ford found him rides in USAC and other car venues. He didn't return to NASCAR until Ford's own boycott of Bill France's regulations in 1966. Desperate for "name" drivers to replace the Fomoco stars who were sidelined, France relented and allowed Turner back into the NASCAR fold. His return to racing ultimately produced a few more wins (bringing his total to seventeen, with money winnings in excess of $118,000), but Turner never recaptured his preban winning form.

It is interesting to note the racing partnership he struck with another famous NASCAR rules breaker, Smokey Yunick, in 1967. By the late-sixties, Smokey had trimmed back his NASCAR efforts to just a handful of superspeedway races where he campaigned his creatively constructed nonfactory-backed Chevrolets. In 1967, Turner and Yunick caused quite a stir when they rolled into the garage area at Daytona just moments before the end of pole qualifying, unloaded a black-and-gold No. 13 Malibu, then broke just about every existing track speed record. When the green flag fell on the 500 that year, it wasn't a factory-backed Chryco or Fomoco on the high-profile pole; instead it was Curtis Turner behind the wheel of Smokey's "independent" Chevelle. Unfortunately, mechanical woes sidelined the car after it had led the race for a considerable period of time. Turner eventually rolled the car into so much scrap metal a few months later during practice for the year's first Atlanta race. Smokey still remembers Turner fondly, though, and contends that he was faster in a race car with a hangover (or worse) than most drivers are while stone cold sober.

Curtis Turner lost his race with life on a foggy Pennsylvania hillside in 1970 when his private plane inexplicably augured into the ground just moments after taking off. Perhaps old rival Bill France had it right when he said at Turner's election to the National Motorsports Press Association Hall of Fame (appropriately housed in the Joe Weatherly Museum trackside in Darlington), that "Curtis Turner was the greatest race car driver I have ever seen."

CHAPTER 20

Darrell Waltrip

Though there isn't a single NASCAR Winston Cup track located within the entire state of Kentucky, you might say that when Darrell Waltrip made his first worldly appearance on February 5, 1947, in Owensboro, he'd been born to race. To his parents Leroy and Margaret's consternation, young Darrell was racing go-karts by the time he was a teenager and had set his sights on a racing career before he had to shave more than twice a week. While in high school, Waltrip excelled as a middle distance runner on the track team and he played basketball as well. But it wasn't stick-and-ball games that captured his interest. No, young Darrell liked going fast. And the racetrack was the only place that he could scratch that itch.

As the oldest of five children in a family of modest means, Waltrip knew that making a place for himself would only come through his own hard work. And fortunately, fate was kind to young

Darrell Waltrip is one of the winningest drivers in NASCAR history. Craft Photo

"DW." For one thing, he was lucky in love. Not only was his future wife, Stevie a beautiful redhead, she also came from a rich family. They married in 1969,

when DW was just twenty-two. After making a name for himself in the Sportsman Division, Waltrip's Winston Cup racing debut came three years later in 1972.

Instead of trying his luck at one of the short tracks on the NASCAR circuit, Waltrip decided to jump in with both feet at Talladega, the fastest track on the entire NASCAR circuit. The race in question was the 1972 Winston 500. His car that day wasn't exactly the class of the field. In fact, it had begun life at Holman and Moody's fabled Charlotte race "factory" fully six years before as a 1967 Fairlane. But not just any Fairlane, you understand. This particular chassis had served Indy star Mario Andretti in his appearance at the Dayton 500 that year. And as most die-hard Ford fans are sure to recall, wee Mario parked the car in Daytona's victory lane that day. During subsequent years, that race car went through a number of hands and more than a few changes. In fact, by 1972 the car had been transformed into a '71 Mercury Cyclone with a Boss 429 engine. When Waltrip pulled into the garage area at Talladega, his car car-

Darrell Waltrip drove his own Mercury during his first outings on the Winston Cup tour. That car had once been
the Fairlane Mario Andretti drove to victory in the '67
Daytona 500. Craft Collection

ried beige, brown, and white No. 95 racing livery
and sponsorship from Stevie's father's company, Terminal Transport. Waltrip qualified the car twenty-fifth
and was sixty-nine laps into the event when his engine gave out.

DW made four more starting fields that year and
managed an eighth-place finish in the Dixie 500 and
a third in Nashville in the Nashville 420. His total
prize money that season was $8,615.

Soon after, Waltrip was driving Chevrolet race
cars and attracting attention. In 1974, for example,
he entered sixteen races and led fourteen. Waltrip's
best finish that year was an impressive second at Darlington in the Southern 500, where he finished one
lap behind Cale Yarborough.

In 1975, Waltrip hired respected crew chief Jake
Elder and boldly predicted that he would win that
season. He did—twice. The first win of DW's Winston
Cup career came, appropriately, at Nashville, his
"home" track, and it came in his fiftieth WC start.
Shortly after that race, Waltrip gave up independent
car ownership for a full-time ride with the Di-Gard
team of Donnie Allison. With the changeover, Wal-

Darrell Waltrip joined Junior Johnson in 1981 and won
his first championship. He drove Mountain Dew Buicks
that year. Craft Collection

Waltrip won his third Winston Cup crown while driving this Junior Johnson-prepared Monte Carlo. Craft Photo

This was Waltrip's home during the '87 NASCAR season. Not exactly comfortable but oh so fast. Craft Photo

Waltrip's Budweiser car was one of many "bubble-back" Chevrolets that ran in 1987. Craft Photo

Waltrip drove for Rick Hendrick next. Different team, same Chevrolet Monte Carlos. Darrell Waltrip won his first Daytona 500 in this Tide-backed Chevrolet. Craft Photo

Waltrip now drives for himself. His Luminas were sponsored by Western Auto in the early nineties. Craft Photo

trip picked up the No. 88, and he posted the first win for the team at Richmond in the Capital City 400.

By 1977, Waltrip was winning regularly on the circuit. He won six times that year, four of them coming on superspeedways, including his first superspeedway win at the Rebel 500 in Darlington. Waltrip also won the Winston 500 that year at Talladega, which perhaps made up for his less-than-impressive first outing there five years earlier.

Waltrip won six more times for Di-Gard in 1978, but it wasn't a congenial year for the team. In fact, by season's end DW wanted out of his contract, but Di-Gard would have nothing of it. Harry Ranier made it known that he wanted Waltrip for his team, but Di-Gard chief Bill Gardner forced Waltrip to stay put and honor his contract (which had four years left to run at the time). Waltrip scored his first win in the World 600 that year, and remained with Di-Gard until he bought his contract out in 1981 for $325,000. Before leaving for Junior Johnson's team, DW won twelve more races for the Di-Gard team.

Nineteen hundred and eighty-one was a standout year for Waltrip. His Junior Johnson-built Buicks carried No. 11 Mountain Dew racing livery and looked good at the head of the pack—which is where they often ran. Waltrip won twelve races that season, including four in a row, and finished in the top ten at thirteen others. Waltrip cinched his first Winston Cup championship at Riverside when he edged out Bobby Allison by finishing sixth in the race.

Waltrip was back in a Johnson-prepped Mountain Dew Buick for 1982, and as in 1981, his primary competition for the WC championship came from Bobby Allison (who, incidentally, drove the Di-Gard Chevrolet). Waltrip won his second straight driving championship by winning twelve races. The title race

Power for Waltrip's racing cars is provided by the same basic Chevrolet small-block engines that Fonty Flock first won a race with in 1955. Craft Photo

While Waltrip's cars are designed to "fly", sometimes they get a bit too high off of the ground. Darrell Waltrip walked away from this wreck in 1991. Craft Photo

again came down to the season finale at Riverside and this time Waltrip finished third behind Allison's second straight win at that event to take the crown by 72 points.

Johnson's team switched to Monte Carlos in 1983 and picked up Pepsi sponsorship. Waltrip survived a horrifying wreck at Daytona (his least favorite track) during the 500. DW was back in winning form by North Wilkesboro and finished the season with six wins. Waltrip stayed with Johnson's organization until 1987, and during the balance of his tenure with the team he posted nineteen more WC wins and won his third driving championship in 1985 when his Kentucky Fried Chicken Monte Carlo edged out Bill Elliott for the crown.

Rick Hendrick was DW's next team owner, and with that switch he picked up the No. 17 and a brilliantly hued Tide backed Monte Carlo. He stayed with Hendrick's multiteam organization through the

1990 season and won his first Daytona 500 in 1989. It was an emotional victory for Waltrip who had tried to win the "big one" for seventeen years.

In 1991, Waltrip set up his own racing facility just south of the Charlotte Motor Speedway. He has campaigned his own Western Auto-sponsored No. 17 Chevrolets ever since. During that time, DW has scored three more wins for himself as a team owner. The first of those came at Pocono in 1992. He also won twice more that season including his first Southern 500 triumph at Darlington. Waltrip's eighty-four NASCAR victories currently place him third on the all-time win list behind Richard Petty and David Pearson. He is currently tied with Bobby Allison for that honored position.

Though at one time reviled by many race fans and called "Jaws" by his fellow competitors, Darrell Waltrip is today one of the most popular and respected drivers on the circuit.

Darrell Waltrip, ahead of the rest. Craft Photo

Chevrolets followed Waltrip's first Mercury and since then he's enjoyed his greatest success as a GM driver. Craft Collection

Darrell Waltrip has spent a lot of time in NASCAR victory lanes. Here, he shares the limelight with Bobby Allison after winning a Daytona 500 qualifier in 1981. Craft Collection

Darrell Waltrip's Western Auto racing colors were shifted to a sleek new Monte Carlo in 1995. The new car's aerodynamic body style aided by the ever-changing NASCAR rules book returned Darrell Waltrip to the head of the pack. Craft Collection

Darrell Waltrip is one of NASCAR's most popular drivers today because he takes time for his fans. Craft Photo

CHAPTER 21

Joe Weatherly

Unlike many of his Grand National counterparts, "Little" Joe Weatherly didn't begin his racing career on four wheels. Motorcycles were Weatherly's first competitive mounts and his 5ft 7in stature served him well in a racing world where a rider's weight is a critical part of the performance package.

Joseph Herbert Weatherly's first work on two wheels came during his tenure as a paper boy in his native Norfolk, Virginia. It's said that as a young man he fell in love with motorcycles because they allowed him to ride tall in the saddle. Born in 1922, Weatherly saw action in World War II as a combat engineer in North Africa and Europe. It was while in Africa that a German sniper added to the character of Weatherly's features by shooting out two of his teeth. Shunts in the AMA motorcycle racing that he took up on his return stateside added their own impressions as well. During the late-1940s, Weatherly was a regular competitor on the mostly dirt track motorcycle circuit, and he achieved a fair amount of fame (and a roomfull of trophies).

In 1950, Little Joe discovered the then-new sport of stock car racing, and he won the first modified

Little Joe Weatherly had been a motorcycle racer of some acclaim before he got interested in stock car racing. That two-wheeled pastime plus a German sniper's bullet left their marks on his face. Weatherly (plaid shirt) is shown here with Cotton Owens, Bud Moore, and modified star, Larry Frank (left to right). The Daytona Racing Archives

race he entered. Soon Weatherly was displaying the same competitive style on four wheels that had produced three AMA motorcycle championships. In 1952, for example, he won forty-nine of eighty-three modified events he entered. He upped that number to fifty-two victories the following year and also took home NASCAR's national modified championship.

When Ford decided to go NASCAR racing in 1956, part of its immense $2million racing budget was devoted to providing Weatherly with a team driver's salary and a fleet of factory-backed convertible division race cars. It was while working for that effort (first for Pete DePaolo and then later in the year for John Holman) that Weatherly first teamed up with Curtis Turner. Though both were Virginians, the casual observer might easily have concluded that the two had little else in common. Weatherly was short, given to wearing saddle shoes, and more than a little fond of practical jokes. Turner, on the other hand, was tall, possessed movie star good looks, and was already a star in the Grand National division. Even so, the two quickly became fast friends—and a dominating force in the all-new convertible division.

Weatherly drove Pontiacs for Bud Moore in 1962 to the Grand National championship. He backed that win up with another in 1963. The Daytona Racing Archives

They also began making selected appearances on the Grand National circuit.

Weatherly finished the 1956 Convertible season fourth in points and third in overall winnings (with purses totaling $18,992). When Holman and Moody was officially formed the following year, Weatherly was one of the first team drivers H&M signed. Though Weatherly had first visited Grand National victory lane in 1956 (at Palm Beach, Florida, and later at Wilson, North Carolina), those two triumphs were subsequently taken away from him by the vagaries of sanctioning body supervision. So it wasn't until August 1958 that Little Joe scored his first official Grand National division victory at a Nashville race that paired GN cars with convertibles such as the 1958 Ford Weatherly drove to victory. All told, Weatherly would rack up twenty-three more GN wins in his career, a figure that still places him twetieth on the NASCAR all-time win list some thirty-odd years after

his death. One of the proudest of those victories came in 1960 at Darlington when he won the Rebel 300, Weatherly's first major victory. Street clothes, shirt-sleeve racing was the order of the day at the time, and Weatherly was often decked out in his "Rebel 300" colored shirt and saddle shoes at subsequent races.

While achieving Grand National division fame, Little Joe also picked up the unofficial title of "The Clown Prince of Automobile Racing" due to his penchant for playing practical jokes and getting into general devilment with his pal, Curtis Turner. Wild parties were a regular part of Weatherly's socializing, as were late-night rental car races on Daytona Beach that were anything but sanctioned by the NASCAR— or the rental agencies. On one particular occasion while Weatherly and Turner were shuttling rental cars full of partying passengers from the airport to a banquet (both drivers owned private planes and were

When team owner Moore switched to Mercurys late in 1964, so did Little Joe. One of Weatherly's Marauders is in the NMPA Joe Weatherly Museum in Darlington today. Craft Collection

among the first on the circuit to fly to and from races), Turner decided to give Weatherly's car a race-track style "pop," and Little Joe quickly responded in kind. By the time the two had reached their destination, both rental cars were total wrecks (as, probably, were the two drivers' helpless passengers!). Neither driver was able to rent a car in that state for a long time thereafter.

Weatherly's greatest success on the circuit came in 1962 and 1963 while driving Pontiacs and Mercurys prepared by legendary car owner Bud Moore. Weatherly had first signed with Moore's Spartanburg, South Carolina, operation in 1961 and was immediately successful, scoring nine wins (among them Old Dominion 500 in Martinsville, the National 400 in Charlotte, and the Southeastern 500 in Bristol) and fourteen top-five finishes. But it was in 1962 that Weatherly and Moore put it all together to win Little Joe's first Grand National driving championship. Powered by Moore's unofficially factory-backed 421 Super Duty Catalina, Weatherly first won that year at Daytona in one of the 500's qualifying races. Fifty-two starts later, Weatherly had turned in one string of nine wins and thirty-nine top-five finishes to clinch the driving championship. His winnings totaled $70,742.10, a paltry amount by today's million-dollar standards, but a significant sum for its time.

Weatherly once again was at the helm of a red-and-black, No. 8 Bud Moore Pontiac in 1963—at least at the outset of the season. It was in 1963 that General Motors withdrew the unofficial factory-backing it had extended to Chevrolet and Pontiac teams throughout the Automobile Manufacturers of America ban (started in 1957) on factory-sponsored motorsports. When Pontiac cut off funding shortly into the 1963 season, Moore was forced to curtail his operations, putting Weatherly on the sidelines at many races. Fortunately, Little Joe was able to "bum" rides at the events Moore couldn't afford to attend, and in so doing kept alive his hopes of a second-straight GN championship. During that season, Weatherly drove for nine different teams, campaigning Pontiacs, Mercurys, Chryslers, and Dodges along the way.

It is obvious from all of this that Weatherly was a tenacious competitor who literally didn't know when to say quit. Graphic evidence of this can be found in his performance at the 1961 Firecracker 250 in Daytona. During that race the transmission in his Pontiac began to kick out of gear without warning—a serious and potentially fatal failure at Daytona even in those days when terminal velocities were "only" in the mid-150mph range. Rather than call it a day, Weatherly chose to twist around in his seat and hold the shifter in gear with his right leg while using his left foot for the gas and brakes. Incredibly, he finished sixth that afternoon.

Weatherly's perseverance paid off for him in 1963 as well. He won three times in a Moore-prepped Pontiac (including a second career Rebel 300 win at Darlington), and thanks to points amassed by his "bummed" rides, clinched the 1963 GN championship behind the wheel of a Moore-built Mercury (with whom Moore had signed late in the season to begin a Fomoco association that continues for his team to this day) at Riverside in the Golden State 400. Weatherly was only the third man in NASCAR history at the time to win back-to-back GN titles (the other two being Buck Baker and Lee Petty).

Unfortunately and tragically, Weatherly's next appearance at Riverside—just two months later—proved to be fatal. Still driving for Moore, whose new Mercury sponsorship permitted running the full GN schedule, Weatherly qualified his red-and-black No. 8 car sixteenth for the road course event. Eighty-six laps into the race, a puff of blue smoke was seen from beneath Weatherly's car just as it was entering Riverside's 180-degree right-hand turn six. A split second later the car crashed heavily, driver's-side-first into the barrier alongside the racing surface. As was his custom, Little Joe wasn't wearing a shoulder harness that day, and, of course, rules mandating window nets were still years in the future. As a result, his head came in contact with the wall during the impact and Weatherly died instantly. Just five months later, Weatherly's former Holman and Moody teammate Fireball Roberts was fatally burned during the World 600. Nineteen hundred and sixty-four was a gloomy year on the circuit, indeed.

Shirt sleeves and saddle shoes were Weatherly's typical driving uniform. He also didn't like to wear a shoulder harness. That fact led directly to his death at Riverside in 1964. The Daytona Racing Archives

The Wood Brothers

Though brothers often go separate ways after reaching their majority, Glen and Leonard Wood have been pursuing the same goal since 1950—winning races. It was in 1950 that the two Stuart, Virginia, boys first conspired to field a stock car (Glen was the driver and kid brother, Leonard, was the mechanic).

Their interest in fast cars, predated that, of course. Their father had been a mechanic, so it was only natural for the two boys to become wrapped up with automobiles. Leonard in particular became fascinated with the workings of a car's mechanics and by the age of fifteen he had progressed from hand-carved model cars to his very first race car. As is the case with many brothers, hand-me-downs were part of the sibling relationship and Leonard's first race car was actually a restoration of big brother Glen's '38 Ford that had been damaged in a towing accident. After putting that car back in racing trim, Leonard was given the job of building all of Glen's racing iron. It was a job that the quiet-spoken Leonard both excelled at and loved.

The Wood Brothers racing team made its first NASCAR outing in 1953 at Martinsville, a track just

The Wood Brothers have been campaigning Fords since Glen's first days as a driver. One of the team's biggest wins came in 1963 when Tiny Lund won the Daytona 500 in storybook fashion. Here, Leonard (left) and Glen (right) celebrate with Tiny in victory lane. The Daytona Racing Archives

25mi west of their home. Glen drove and Leonard turned the wrenches on the Wood Brothers' '53 Lincoln sporting No. 21. Though Glen finished a dismal thirtieth that day, in the years to come the two brothers would make the No. 21 a regular fixture in NASCAR victory lanes.

When Grand National success was not immediately forthcoming, Glen and Leonard focused on the modified circuit, where Glen made a name for himself as a promising young driver. When NASCAR formed the convertible division in 1956, the Wood Brothers were one of the earliest teams to field a car. Their first drop top appearance came at Greensboro, where Glen finished third. By the end of that first convertible season, Glen had posted fourteen more top-five finishes and was tenth in the final season championship. Convertible victory No. 1 came for the Wood Brothers team at the third race of the 1957 season in Fayetteville, North Carolina. Glen won three more times that year, as always at the wheel of a Ford product, and finished third in points behind Joe Weatherly and Bob Welborn. When younger brother Leonard was drafted in 1957, Glen continued to race for the team without him.

Glen won one more convertible race while Leonard was away (in 1958) and turned in several top-five finishes.

A return to the Grand National ranks came next in 1959, and Glen's '58 Ford convertible qualified eighth for the inaugural running of the Daytona 500. Luck wasn't with him that day and a blown clutch sidelined the car on lap 149. With Leonard freshly returned in 1960 from his duty in Germany, the Wood Brothers began to provide rides for drivers like Speedy Thompson, Joe Weatherly, Junior Johnson, and Curtis Turner (a fellow Virginian who'd played a large role in the Woods' decision to pursue a racing career), as well as for Glen.

The team's first Grand National win came at Winston Salem when Glen beat Chevrolet driver Rex White to the stripe in a 50mi event. Glen won a second race in 1960, and Speedy Thompson provided the team's first major victory by putting a No. 21 Wood Brothers Ford in victory lane at the first running of the National 500 in Charlotte.

When Ford rediscovered NASCAR racing in 1962, the Wood Brother's steadfast and true Ford team was one of the first to be plugged back into the factory money pipeline. When that happened, Marvin Panch was signed as team driver. Glen eventually hung up his helmet after recording his fourth and final Grand National win at Winston Salem in 1963.

During the 1963 season, the Wood Brothers were involved in a story that rivaled anything ever scripted by a Hollywood writer. The race in question was the 1963 Daytona 500, and, as in 1962, Marvin Panch had been signed to drive for the team. Luck was not with Panch that year and he became involved in a serious accident at the speedway just ten days before the race while testing a "Bird Cage" Maserati. As the wreckage of the car ground to a halt upside down, an intense fire erupted. Pinned inside the overturned and blazing car, things were looking bleak for Panch until Dewayne "Tiny" Lund rushed to his rescue.

Lund, a journeyman racer on the modified and GN circuits, was actually a much larger man than his nickname implied. Fact of the matter was, he was built more like Paul Bunyan. Sprinting to the car before track safety crews could arrive, Lund almost single-handedly lifted the blazing sports car off Panch and effected his escape. Though injured seriously enough to be hospitalized, Panch would live to race another day thanks to Tiny's heroism. When he asked the Woods to consider Tiny as his replacement in the 500, they quickly agreed. Tiny qualified the team's Galaxie twelfth and then relied on the Woods' pit strategy to win the race. He crossed the finish line out of gas but ahead of second-place finisher Fred Lorenzen. Once in victory lane, Tiny did just what any farm-raised Iowa boy might do—he let out a hog call. It was a popular win and shortly after the race, Lund received the Carnegie Medal for Heroism.

Cale Yarborough was another driver who found great success in a Wood Brothers-prepared car. He drove a team Mercury to victory in the 1968 Daytona 500. The Daytona Racing Archives

As mentioned, it was the Wood Brothers, pit strategy that won the 1963 Daytona 500. It was also pit strategy that made the team famous all across the circuit. In the early days of stock car racing, pit stops were often leisurely affairs, and on some occasions drivers were known to leave their cars during a service stop to have a sandwich. Leonard and Glen were two of the first on the Grand National tour to realize that a race could actually be won in the pits, and they began to concentrate their efforts on making service stops—especially those under green flag conditions—more expeditious.

Working with a pit crew composed of their brothers Delano and Clay, along with a collection of other relatives and friends, the team worked hard at perfecting race-condition pit stops. While other teams didn't take pit work seriously, by the mid-sixties the Wood Brothers had reduced the time it took to change four tires and fill the tank to a then-incredible twenty-five seconds. The sixteen-second pit stops that are common along pit road today are a direct outgrowth of the Wood Brothers' early attention to that vitally important aspect of NASCAR racing. Fact is, the team became so famous for its pit work that corporate sponsor Ford hired the Woods to pit for

Yarborough also drove long-nosed Spoiler IIs for the Woods in 1969 and '70. The victories he won for those two seasons helped Ford win the factory-backed Aero-Wars. These victories were aided by the Wood Brothers, innovation of making pit stops a lightning-quick affair. The Daytona Racing Archives

Jimmy Clark's Lotus Ford team at the Indy 500 in 1964 and 1965, and they played an instrumental role in the Scot's 1965 Brickyard victory.

In addition to providing cars for Panch (until 1966), the Woods also hosted sports car racer Dan Gurney when the tour trekked to the Riverside road course in California. The wins he scored there are in large part attributable to their pit work and mechanical support.

Following the end of Ford's series boycott in 1966 (due to a dispute about the legality of that manufacturer's new 427 SOHC engine), Cale Yarborough joined the Wood Brothers team. In 1966 and 1967, the diminutive South Carolinian drove factory-backed Fairlanes for the team to wins in the Atlanta 500 and the Firecracker 400. But it was in 1968 that the combination really began to cook. Following corporate orders, the Woods switched to Mercury that year and fielded the all-new Cyclone body style. The car's new exaggerated fastback roofline turned out to be nearly perfect for superspeedway work. When powered by a fire-breathing, twin four-barrel-inducted 427 Tunnel Port engine, the car was able to run nearly 190mph. In fact, Yarborough put the red-and-white Wood Brothers, Mercury on the pole at Day-

Leonard Wood's skill with a wrench has produced many NASCAR victories. Craft Photo

tona that year with a qualifying speed of 189.22mph before handily winning the race. Yarborough's only real competition that day was similarly named LeeRoy Yarbrough, also in a Cyclone. The rest of the season was pretty much a Cale and LeeRoy fundraiser, and between them they decided most of the tour's superspeedway events. Cale accounted for six wins in 1968, including victories at the Firecracker 400 and the Southern 500.

When the factory-backed Aero-Wars broke out in 1969, Yarborough's Cyclone grew an extended nose to become even faster. Especially when powered by the all-new 429ci Hemi engines that Fomoco unveiled at Atlanta that season. Yarborough proved as much when he drove his new Boss 429-powered Cyclone Spoiler II to victory at the Atlanta 500 and the Motor State 500 at Michigan. Though Ford emasculated its racing budget for 1970 (before retreating from the NASCAR series altogether in 1971), Yarborough and the Woods were still able to post super-

speedway wins that year at a Daytona 500 qualifier, the Motor State 400 (reduced 100mi from the 1969 race) and the American 500 in Rockingham. When NASCAR ended the Aero-Wars with a rules book change in 1971, Spoiler II and Talladega drivers like Yarborough had won the conflict with twenty-two superspeedway victories, eight more than their radically winged Mopar adversaries.

Donnie Allison and A.J. Foyt drove for the Woods after Cale left. The team reverted to the "regular-nosed" '68 Cyclone body style they had used earlier, and A.J. ran third in the 1971 Daytona 500. Two weeks later, his No. 21 Merc was in victory lane at Ontario, a California track that had been built as a replica of the Indianapolis Motor Speedway. A.J. also won at Atlanta that season, and Allison won for the Woods at Talladega in May.

Nineteen hundred and seventy-two saw the start of a string of superspeedway wins for the Wood, who actually won more races than ever before after decid-

1988 CITGO/WOOD BROTHERS RACING TEAM

GLEN WOOD-CAR OWNER

LEONARD WOOD-CREW CHEIF

EDDIE WOOD-MECHANIC

(L to R) LEN WOOD, GLEN WOOD, LEONARD WOOD, EDDIE WOOD

LEN WOOD-MECHANIC

The Wood Brothers' team today includes Glen's sons, Eddie and Len. They'll keep the family name in the winner's circle for years to come. Craft Collection

While other teams have moved to Charlotte and huge facilities, the Woods still use the same modestly sized shop they've had since the sixties. Craft Photo

ing to run only at select superspeedway races. Foyt returned as team driver and he got the year off to a good start by winning the Daytona 500 in the team's new '71 Cyclone body style car. Though not readily apparent, Mercury's 1970 and 1971 Cyclone was actually a very aerodynamic race car, and with Woods Brothers preparation, it was nearly unbeatable on superspeedways. Foyt won again for the team at Ontario before returning to the Indy car ranks. That's when David Pearson began his fabled seven-year association with the team.

He began by winning the Rebel 400 for the team at Darlington and didn't stop until he had parked his No. 21 Mercury in victory lane forty-three more times. Of those wins, fully twenty-four were secured by Pearson while at the wheel of a 1971 Mercury Cyclone. It was an incredible race car and, of course, Pearson was an incredible race car driver.

Pearson and the Woods parted company in 1979 after a pit miscue at Darlington caused him to head back into the race before all four wheels had been secured. He made it as far as the exit of pit lane before two wheels left the car for good. Their exit signaled Pearson's own departure and soon Neil Bonnett was the new Wood Brothers driver. Bonnett,

close friend of the Allisons and a member of the "Alabama Gang," won for the Woods at Pocono and Talladega in 1980. In 1981, he won the Southern 500 for the team in a new downsized "Fox"-bodied Thunderbird, and also finished first at Dover and Atlanta. Bonnett posted one more win for the team at the 1982 World 600 before giving up his seat to Buddy Baker in 1983. Amiable but rough on machinery, Baker gave the Woods just one victory—the 1983 Firecracker 400—before he in turn was replaced by "the King's" young son, Kyle Petty in 1985. Petty earned his first two Winston Cup trophies while driving Wood Brothers' Thunderbirds in 1986 and 1987.

Five years passed before another second-generation driver, Dale Jarrett, would show the team the way-back to the winner's circle at the fall 1991 Michigan race. The team's most recent win came at Atlanta in May 1993, courtesy of driver Morgan Shepherd.

In recent years, more and more of the team's operation has been handed over to Glen's sons, Eddie and Len. With their guidance, it's likely that the Wood Brothers racing team of Stuart, Virginia, will be recording Ford wins for another four decades.

Chapter 23

Cale Yarborough

If ever Grand National (nee Winston Cup) stock car racing had a Horatio Alger story, it would have to be about the career of William Caleb Yarborough. That's because in the course of just a handful of years, the stocky Sardis, South Carolina, native went from being so desperate to be involved in racing that he swept floors at Holman and Moody, to ranking fifth on the all-time NASCAR win list with eighty-three victories.

Cale was born in March 1939 in an unpainted frame house that lacked indoor plumbing. His early years were a mixture of tobacco farming with his family and dreaming about the goings-on just down the road in Darlington at the superspeedway that opened there in 1950. When the engines roared to life for the first Southern 500 that year, young Cale was there—but not as a paying customer. The youngster had snuck into the track and watched the race from a perch on the grandstand's chicken wire fencing. The seeds of desire were planted in Yarborough that day and his ambition was to become a race car driver.

After getting his first break with Banjo Matthews, Cale Yarborough signed on with the Wood Brothers. Craft Collection

Yarborough financed those aspirations in a number of ways. A calf he raised to maturity provided the money for his first car. Later he bought junked cars from a local scrap yard to repair and sell for a profit. When finances allowed, he campaigned his own home-built cars on the local dirt track bull rings near Hartsville and Sumter, South Carolina.

Yarborough's first foray into the NASCAR big leagues came in 1957 when he was just sixteen and he drove in the Southern 500. Though unable to officially enter the race because of his young age, Yarborough made a deal with a friend who had qualified a Pontiac for the race. When NASCAR inspectors weren't looking, Yarborough slipped into the car and joined the race. He ultimately finished enough laps to be ranked in the forty-second finishing position—ahead of series regulars like Fonty Flock and Paul Goldsmith—and earned his first Grand National purse: $100. Before his career as a driver was over Yarborough would add more than $5million dollars in winnings to that figure.

Yarborough had a fantastic year with the Wood Brothers in 1968 and won many superspeedway races. Craft Collection

Yarborough's 427-powered Mercury was one of the winningest cars in the Grand National Division in 1968. Craft Collection

Unfortunately, his first venture into the NASCAR ranks did not immediately produce a regular ride. In fact, Cale endured years of hard times and a variety of odd jobs before getting a big break. Among the trades he pursued in the interim were logging, semi-pro football, and turkey farming. All the while, he never lost sight of his goal and raced whenever possible. One time, funds were so tight that he and his wife had to scour their car's seat cushions to come up with the 50 cents bridge toll necessary for Cale to make it to a track to race. As luck would have it, the Yarboroughs could only come up with 37 cents, but the toll keeper took pity on them and let them pass. On the way home from the race, Yarborough made a point of repaying the 13 cents he owed.

Yarborough's luck began to change in August 1964 when Ford racing chief Jacque Passino offered him a try-out for a new team car Holman and Moody were to run at Ashville-Weaverville, North Carolina, Speedway. Though engine failure relegated Yarborough to a twentieth place finish, he was invited by

Yarborough won his first Daytona 500 in 1968. Craft Collection

In 1969, Cale drove swoopy Cyclone Spoiler IIs. They were fast. Here Cale (right) and David Pearson (left) lead the pack out of turn four at Daytona. Ford Archives Photo

Cale Yarborough (right) and Donnie Allison (left) were two of the hottest drivers on the circuit from 1968 to 1970. The Daytona Racing Archives

John Holman to come to Charlotte and work at H&M. Yarborough's first tasks for H&M included sweeping floors and being a general "gopher," for which he was paid the princely sum of $1.25 an hour. In 1965, he hitched several rides in a '64 Ford provided by Kenny Myler, and he scored his first GN victory in a 100mi dirt track race at Valdosta, Georgia. Yarborough got the chance to drive Banjo Matthew's factory-backed '65 Galaxie at several events in 1965. His best finish was a second behind Curtis Turner in the American 500 at Rockingham. Yarborough's performance on the track did not go unnoticed back at Holman and Moody, and his hourly salary was increased to $1.75.

The year 1966 started auspiciously for Yarborough with a second-place finish in the Daytona 500 in Banjo Matthews' Ford-backed '66 Galaxie. But even that impressive performance, coupled with a handful of other top-five finishes, didn't immediately

translate into a full-time ride. Late in the season, however, the Wood Brothers hired him to drive their No. 21 Galaxie in the Southern 500—just down the way from Cale's boyhood home. Because NASCAR is not very much like Hollywood (just watch *Days of Thunder* if you have any doubts), Yarborough did not win the race that day. In fact, he finished well off of the pace in eleventh. Even so, that first pairing with the famed Wood Brothers' Stuart, Virginia, team was a harbinger of good things to come.

In 1967, Yarborough had a full-time ride with the team and enjoyed Ford factory-backing. He posted a superspeedway win at Atlanta in the Atlanta 500 (which he went on to win for three years in a row and six times during his career). In July, he won his second superspeedway title by edging out Dick Hutcherson in the Firecracker 400. At season's end, Yarborough had added fourteen more top-ten finishes and claimed more than $57,000 in winnings.

If 1967 was good to Cale, then 1968 was absolutely fantastic. He teamed once again with the Wood Brothers, who that year made a switch to the all-new-for-1968 fastback-rooflined Mercury Montego. Though still powered by the 427 Tunnel Port engines that had "motorvated" Yarborough's stubby little Fairlanes the season before, the Montego's slippery new silhouette had the same effect as adding extra cubic inches under the hood, and Yarborough quickly capitalized on that aerodynamic advantage. In Daytona 500 time trials, he upped the track's qualifying record speed to 189.222mph (9mph faster than Curtis Turner's pole speed 1966). In the 500 itself, Yarborough averaged 143.251mph on his way to his first (of four in his career) 500 victory and the $47,250 purse. Yarborough won five more times that year (including Atlanta 500 and Firecracker 400 victories), but perhaps the most rewarding triumph of all came in September when he edged out Holman and Moody driver (and eventual GN champ) David Pearson to win the 1968 Southern 500—the race he'd snuck in to see back in 1950.

When the Aero-Wars broke out between Fomoco and Chryco in 1969, Yarborough went to "war" in the Wood Brothers' super-slippery, long-nosed version of the Montego, referred to as the Cyclone Spoiler II. Graced with the best aerodynamics of the new crop of Fomoco and Mopar aero cars that year, Yarborough's fastback Mercurys got even faster when the all-new Boss 429 Hemi-headed engine was introduced at Atlanta. In fact, his red-and-white No. 21 car was often the fastest on the track, a point he underscored by convincingly winning the Atlanta 500. Yarborough campaigned his long-nosed Spoiler for two seasons, scoring five more wins with the car.

Yarborough parted company with the Wood Brothers in 1971 following Ford's decision to pull out of factory-backed racing. For the next two years he focused on the Indy car circuit—but that's another story. He returned to the now-Winston Cup stock car ranks in 1973 and joined forces with Junior Johnson, who had switched to Chevrolet when Ford withdrew from racing. Though Chevy had been on the NASCAR sidelines since 1963, Johnson and a young, former Holman and Moody mechanic named Robert Yates had figured out how to make a big-block-powered Chevelle fly, and in Cale they found the perfect pilot.

The new team struck first blood at the Southeastern 500 in Bristol and won three more times (including Yarborough's second Southern 500 win) before ending up second in the season's points race. It was the first of eight successful seasons that Yarborough, Johnson, and Chevrolet would spend together. Along the way, that troika won fifty-five Winston Cup races and an incredible and unprecedented three straight national driving championships in a row (1976, 1977, and 1978).

Yarborough next joined forces with car owner M.C. Anderson, and then Harry Ranier, who both fielded GM-based (Chevrolet, Pontiac, and Buick) race teams, and scored fourteen more victories for the "General" through the 1984 season.

Perhaps the most notable of those came in 1983 at Daytona, where Yarborough scored his third Daytona 500 win. What made that triumph so remarkable was the wild ride that Cale had taken just days before the race. Just after officially breaking the 200mph barrier in a stock car for the first time, his No. 28 Monte Carlo became airborne, then tore itself to shreds in the ensuing shunt. Miraculously, Cale escaped serious injury. Even more of a surprise was the win he scored over Bill Elliott in the 500 while driving the Ranier team's back-up Pontiac.

After nearly fifteen years away from Ford race cars, Yarborough returned to the fold in 1985, when the Ranier team switched manufacturers. He scored

In the early and mid-seventies, Junior Johnson and Cale Yarborough teamed up to dominate the NASCAR circuit. The Chevrolets and Oldsmobiles they campaigned were always the class of the field. Craft Collection

After hanging up his driving gloves for good, Yarborough became a car owner. His first cars were Pontiacs. He later shifted racing allegiances to Ford. Craft Collection

two more of Ford's all-time leading (as this is written) 424 NASCAR victories before setting out on his own as a team owner in 1987. When Cale took that big step for his last two years as a driver, he returned to the GM cars that had served him so well during the seventies and eighties. In 1988, Cale hung up his helmet for good and shifted exclusively to the role that he still occupies today of team owner.

When asked about the way to drive a race car, Yarborough once said, "There's only one way to dri-ve as far as I'm concerned, and that's flat out. If you don't charge from the start, there are plenty of great drivers around who will." And that's pretty much exactly what Cale Yarborough did during his thirty-one years on the NASCAR circuit. How else could one man win eighty-three of the 559 races he started, including fifty superspeedway titles and a record five Southern 500s at Darlington, the toughest track on the circuit?

CHAPTER 24

Smokey Yunick

You might say that they broke the mold when Henry Smokey Yunick was born. And even if they didn't, Smokey has spent most of the years since his birth in 1923 making damned sure that the racing world would never know another like him.

You see, Smokey usually prefers making his own rules to following someone else's. What's really perplexing about that trait is that Smokey is usually right. Especially when it comes to things mechanical.

Though born in Tennessee, Smokey spent his boyhood years north of the Mason-Dixon line in Pennsylvania. Many of his earliest years were spent on the family farm in exceedingly close proximity to the southern end of a north bound horse. That is, until Smokey grew weary of that particular view at age thirteen and decided to rebuild a junkyard tractor. He's been tinkering with machinery ever since.

By the age of fourteen he was working full time in a garage for $5 a

Smokey Yunick is considered by many to be one of the greatest racing mechanics of all time. The Daytona Racing Archives

week, and shortly thereafter he took up the sport of motorcycle racing. Still just plain Henry Yunick at the time, one particular racing bike he owned had more than a little trouble keeping oil out of the combus-

tion chamber. The end result was a plume of pollution that followed Yunick all the way around the track. Before long, his on-track rivals started calling him "Smokey," and the nickname stuck.

When World War II came up, Smokey volunteered for the Army Air Corp and ultimately was commissioned a second lieutenant. Though only in possession of ten years of formal education, Yunick breezed through flight school and was assigned to B-17 Flying Fortress duty. When a medical problem temporarily delayed his deployment to a combat bomber squadron, Yunick was assigned to flying check-out runs in B-17s undergoing repair.

Some of those flights took him far down the Florida peninsula and he was struck at the time by the beauty of Daytona Beach from the air. As racing fans will already know, that's just where Yunick settled after the war to open up what he called the "Best Damn Garage in Town." But not before he had racked up an impressive war record of fifty-two bombing missions all across Europe, Africa, and Indochina in a Flying Fortress named "Smokey and His Fireman."

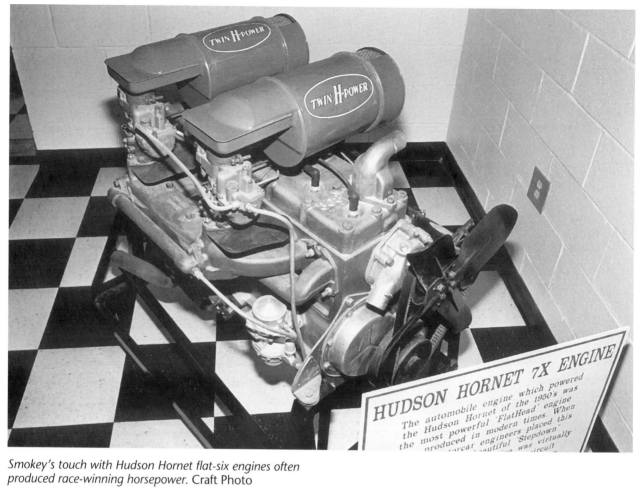

Smokey's touch with Hudson Hornet flat-six engines often produced race-winning horsepower. Craft Photo

Back in civilian life, Smokey decided to leave the "great white north" for the balmier climes of Florida, and he pulled his trailer to Daytona. His first garage there was a shop shared with a blacksmith. But before long Smokey's mechanical skill produced the capital necessary to open up his own truck repair shop. With Daytona serving as the center for motorsports in postwar America, it seemed only natural for Smokey to eventually get caught up in the business of building race cars. Yunick's first work on four-wheeled racing machinery came in 1947, when he started working on the Fords of Daytona racer Marshall Teague. When Teague, an early star on the NASCAR circuit, switched to Hudson Hornets in 1951, Smokey also made the switch and soon Yunick-prepared Hornets were powering Teague and Herb Thomas to dirt track victories all across the country. Fonty Flock, his brother Tim, Paul Goldsmith, Curtis Turner, Ralph Moody, and Junior Johnson all drove cars that Yunick either owned or prepared during NASCAR's first decade. All told, Yunick's cars finished first fifty-two times in that period.

When the Hudsons were passed by in the race for even more performance, Smokey switched his ef-

forts to making GM cars go faster—especially cars of the Chevrolet persuasion. In fact, it was Yunick who, with the help of driver Herb Thomas, provided the motivation for Chevrolet's first superspeedway win in the NASCAR ranks at the 1955 Southern 500 in Darlington.

Though most strongly associated with Chevrolet racing cars, Yunick has also campaigned Fords and Pontiacs. His first stint with Ford came in 1957, when the Blue Oval company hired him to field a team of factory Fords alongside those being built by Holman and Moody. Though he and driver Paul Goldsmith (who was, according to Smokey, the best natural driver he ever saw) found success quickly with their supercharged (that's right—1957 NASCAR Fords ran supercharged engines!) Fairlanes, Yunick's tenure with Ford was abruptly ended by that manufacturer's ill-advised decision to withdraw from factory-backed motorsports.

With Ford on the sidelines, Smokey switched to Pontiac, whose racing division door was still wide open despite the ban. All told, Yunick's black-and-gold Ponchos won four of the first eight superspeedway events held at Daytona, including 500 wins scored by Marvin Panch and Fireball Roberts in 1961 and 1962, respectively. Along the way Yunick developed a reputation for stretching the official rule book as far as it would go (and in some cases a good deal further). He also became embroiled in a feud with Bill France's NASCAR bureaucracy that is still the basis for hard feelings between Smokey and the NASCAR powers that be today.

All manner of rules violations have been attributed to Smokey over the years. Perhaps the rules he actually *did* break were more the result of his innovation rather than any conscious desire to thwart the sanctioning body's wishes. On the other hand, as far as Smokey was concerned, as long as the rules book didn't specifically *forbid* something that meant it was perfectly OK to do it.

Keeping in mind that NASCAR's earliest rules books were anything-but-comprehensive one-page affairs, you can begin to understand the leeway that Smokey's view of the world permitted in terms of mechanical ingenuity.

Smokey's aircraft background, for example, made him one of the first car builders to realize the

Smokey called his shop "The Best Damn Garage in Town" and painted that logo on most cars built there. Craft Photo

Smokey has built just about every kind of race car there is, but is most often linked with Chevrolets. The Chevelles he built from '66 to '68 became NASCAR legends. Craft Photo

Yunick's Chevelles were blisteringly fast. Here, Curtis Turner leads the pack at Daytona. Craft Collection

Smokey rejoined Ford for 1969 and campaigned Torino Talladegas. Charlie Glotzbach was one of the drivers who drove a Smokey-prepped Big T that year. The Daytona Racing Archives

power of aerodynamics. As early as 1952, he was "Bondo-ing" up the exposed frame members beneath his Hudson Hornets to smooth air flow under the cars. Smokey tried destroked engines (for more rpms), power steering, fuel cells, on-board hydraulic jacks (for faster pit stops), and on-board fire systems well before other mechanics on the circuit thought of them. As a result of being ahead of the mechanical learning curve, Yunick's innovations were often summarily banned by the sanctioning doges—only to become "legal" several years later when the rest of the racing world had caught up.

Of course, there were occasions when Smokey actually *did* set out to defeat the rules book. Perhaps the best examples of these mechanical transgressions were the 1966 Chevelle Malibus that he built for use in the 1966 through 1968 Daytona and Atlanta superspeedway races. By the mid-sixties, Yunick had curtailed his racing activities to only a handful of selected races, usually those held at Daytona and Atlanta. The Chevelles he built for Mario Andretti, Curtis Turner, and Indy star Gordon Johncock to campaign during the mid-sixties were perhaps some of the trickiest race cars ever built. As a result, they have become the stuff of NASCAR legend.

Take the Chevelle that Smokey brought to Atlanta in 1966 during the abortive Ford boycott of the series (due to Bill France's refusal to legalize the 427 SOHC motor for competition). According to racing lore, the diminutive Chevy was built curiously underscale—approximately 15/16, according to some reports. But NASCAR, desperate for a draw with most Ford teams on the sidelines, still permitted the car to run. According to Smokey, there was nothing downsized about the car at all, and to prove his point, he built one of the first body templates used in NASCAR to compare its silhouette favorably with a rental car leased at the Atlanta airport.

Even so, the myth of Smokey's 15/16ths Chevy persists to this day. Curtis Turner didn't make the racing establishment (the Chryco and Fomoco factory sponsors) very happy one year later when he and Smokey conspired to win the very high-profile pole position for the 1967 Daytona 500 with yet another independently campaigned Chevelle. Smokey's secret that year was to build a 427 big-block engine that actually displaced a mere 410ci. The theory was that the lighter reciprocating assembly would permit higher backstretch revs (read: speed) with less punishment to the engine. Smokey and Turner made their first appearance at the track that year just an hour or so before the track closed on pole qualifying day. Without wasting time, they unloaded the little No. 13 Chevelle and Turner headed onto the track.

A handful of laps later, Turner had shattered the old lap record with an average speed of 180.831mph—a speed fully 5mph faster than 1966 pole winner Richard Petty's best effort one year before. The assembled Ford and Chryco racers who had been flogging their cars for a week in anticipation of pole day were, not surprisingly, fit to be tied—and so were their corporate sponsors back home in Detroit. Fortunately for their corporate egos, Turner, whose only throttle position was flat on the floor, grenaded the destroked motor on lap 143.

If Smokey had a mechanical masterpiece it would have to be the '66 Chevelle he built for Gordon Johncock for the 1968 Daytona 500. It was so sophisticated a piece of engineering that volumes of hyperbole would still fail to do it justice. In short, it represented everything that Smokey had learned about building a race car during his lengthy career. Built over a hand-fabricated tubular frame years before that style of chassis became a fixture on the circuit, the black-and-gold Chevelle possessed a myriad of semilegal, er, enhancements, all designed to improve performance.

From the sectioned front bumper that served as an airfoil, to the shallow vortex generator scooped out of the car's roofline (to better direct the air toward the rear deck spoiler), to the way the entire car sat back and to the left of the frame's centerline (for better weight distribution in the turns), the car was a mechanical marvel.

As a result, the NASCAR officials of the day never let it run even one lap at Daytona (or anywhere else,

Though in semiretirement today, Smokey's shop is still a favorite stop for racing enthusiasts during every Daytona speed week. Craft Photo

Smokey is still fond of his trademark "flat-top" Stetson head gear. His formal toppers carry substantially less motor oil than his shop versions. Craft Photo

for that matter). When it became obvious that the deck had been stacked against him by Bill France and his legion of tech inspectors, Yunick, in a fit of rage, sloshed a few gallons of gas in the car and drove it back to his Beach Street shop—through traffic! The headlines in the next day's paper claimed the car had been driven home without its gas tank, and yet another legend was born.

When Smokey's corporate mentor, Semon "Bunkie" Knudsen left GM for Ford in 1969, Yunick once again found himself working for the Blue Oval. His duties that year included campaigning a super-swoopy, Boss 429-powered Torino Talladega and an equally new and innovative Boss 302 Mustang (in NASCAR's Grand American series for pony cars). In a way, his participation in the 1969 Aero-Wars (where Ford and Chryco introduced specially bodied aerodynamically enhanced race cars) was a vindication of Smokey's early interest in race car aerodynamics. It also represented one of the last times he campaigned a car in the Grand National ranks. When Knudsen was summarily fired by Ford in 1970, thereby mortally wounding the corporation's racing efforts, Yunick left its employment, too.

Though out of NASCAR competition since 1970, Smokey Yunick is still regarded as one of the greatest racing mechanics of all times. Every year when the NASCAR circus returns to Daytona, his "Best Damn Garage in Town" attracts scores of supplicants in the same way the Mecca draws the Muslim faithful.

NASCAR Grand National/ Winston Cup Victories 1949–1994

Driver	Victories		
Richard Petty	200	Mark Martin	14
David Pearson	105	Dick Rathman	13
Bobby Allison	84	Tim Richmond	13
Darrell Waltrip	84	Terry Labonte	13
Cale Yarborough	83	Ernie Irvan	12
Dale Earnhardt	63	Donnie Allison	10
Lee Petty	54	Paul Goldsmith	9
Ned Jarrett	50	Cotton Owens	9
Junior Johnson	50	Kyle Petty	7
Herb Thomas	49	Marshall Teague	7
Buck Baker	46	Bob Welborn	7
Tim Flock	40	Jim Reed	7
Bill Elliott	40	A.J. Foyt	7
Rusty Wallace	39	Darel Dieringer	6
Bobby Isaac	37	Alan Kulwicki	5
Fireball Roberts	32	Ralph Moody	5
Rex White	26	Dan Gurney	5
Fred Lorenzen	26	Dave Marcis	5
Jim Paschal	25	Pete Hamilton	4
Joe Weatherly	24	Bob Flock	4
Jack Smith	21	Hershel McGriff	4
Benny Parsons	21	Lloyd Dane	4
Fonty Flock	19	Ed Pagan	4
Speedy Thompson	19	Eddie Gray	4
Buddy Baker	19	Glen Wood	4
Davey Allison	19	Nelson Stacy	4
Neil Bonnett	18	Billy Wade	4
Harry Gant	18	Morgan Shepherd	4
Curtis Turner	17	Charlie Glotzbach	4
Marvin Panch	17	Parnelli Jones	4
Geoff Bodine	17	Ken Schrader	4
Ricky Rudd	15	Dick Linder	3
Dick Hutcherson	14	Frank Mundy	3
LeeRoy Yarbrough	14	Bill Blair	3
		Gwyn Staley	3

Driver	Victories
Dale Jarrett	3
Derrike Cope	2
Tiny Lund	2
Red Byron	2
Gober Sosebee	2
Danny Letner	2
Billy Myers	2
Marvin Porter	2
Johnny Beauchamp	2
Tom Pistone	2
Bobby Johns	2
Emanuel Zervakis	2
Jim Pardue	2
Elmo Langley	2
James Hylton	2
Ray Elder	2
Joe Lee Johnson	2
Tommy Thompson	2
Jimmy Spencer	2
Jeff Gordon	2
Brett Bodine	1
Greg Sacks	1
Bobby Hillin	1
Phil Parsons	1
Lake Speed	1
Jody Ridley	1
Bob Burdick	1
Neil Cole	1
Marvin Burke	1
Denny Weinberg	1
Bill Norton	1
Buddy Norton	1
Buddy Shuman	1
Dick Passwater	1
Al Keller	1
John Soares, Sr.	1
Chuck Stevenson	1
Johnny Kieper	1
Royce Hagerty	1
Art Watts	1
Bill Amick	1
Danny Graves	1
Frankie Schneider	1
Shorty Rollins	1
Jim Cook	1
Jim Roper	1
June Cleveland	1
Jack White	1
Harold Kite	1
Bill Rexford	1
Johnny Mantz	1
Leon Sales	1
Lloyd Moore	1
Joe Eubanks	1
John Rostek	1
Johnny Allen	1
Larry Frank	1
Johnny Rutherford	1
Wendell Scott	1
Sam McQuagg	1
Paul Lewis	1
Earl Balmer	1
Jim Hurtubise	1
Mario Andretti	1
Richard Brickhouse	1
Mark Donohue	1
Dick Brooks	1
Earl Ross	1
Lou Figaro	1
Jim Florian	1
Lennie Pond	1
Ron Bouchard	1
Sterling Marlin	1

APPENDIX B

NASCAR Grand National/ Winston Cup Champions 1949–1994

1949	Red Byron	1972	Richard Petty
1950	Bill Rexford	1973	Benny Parsons
1951	Herb Thomas	1974	Richard Petty
1952	Tim Flock	1975	Richard Petty
1953	Herb Thomas	1976	Cale Yarborough
1954	Lee Petty	1977	Cale Yarborough
1955	Tim Flock	1978	Cale Yarborough
1956	Buck Baker	1979	Richard Petty
1957	Buck Baker	1980	Dale Earnhardt
1958	Lee Petty	1981	Darrell Waltrip
1959	Lee Petty	1982	Darrell Waltrip
1960	Rex White	1983	Bobby Allison
1961	Ned Jarrett	1984	Terry Labonte
1962	Joe Weatherly	1985	Darrell Waltrip
1963	Joe Weatherly	1986	Dale Earnhardt
1964	Richard Petty	1987	Dale Earnhardt
1965	Ned Jarrett	1988	Bill Elliott
1966	David Pearson	1989	Rusty Wallace
1967	Richard Petty	1990	Dale Earnhardt
1968	David Pearson	1991	Dale Earnhardt
1969	David Pearson	1992	Alan Kulwicki
1970	Bobby Isaac	1993	Dale Earnhardt
1971	Richard Petty	1994	Dale Earnhardt

Index